Development and Assessment of 30-Meter Pine Density Maps for Landscape-Level Modeling of Mountain Pine Beetle Dynamics

Benjamin A. Crabb, James A. Powell, and Barbara J. Bentz

United States Department of Agriculture / Forest Service

Rocky Mountain Research Station

Research Paper RMRS-RP-93WWW

July 2012

Abstract

Forecasting spatial patterns of mountain pine beetle (MPB) population success requires spatially explicit information on host pine distribution. We developed a means of producing spatially explicit datasets of pine density at 30-m resolution using existing geospatial datasets of vegetation composition and structure. Because our ultimate goal is to model MPB population success, three study areas in the western United States that have experienced recent MPB outbreaks were used for evaluation. Pine density estimates for each study area were compared to measures of cumulative MPB-caused pine mortality summarized from annual Aerial Detection Surveys (ADS). ADS data provide spatial and temporal representations of MPB-caused pine mortality collected by observers in fixed wing aircraft and are the most readily available estimates of landscape-scale impacts of MPB. Regression analyses using LANDFIRE ecological systems classifications (EVTs) as units of analysis showed that the best pine density estimates explained 75 to 98% of cumulative MPB-caused tree mortality. LANDFIRE EVTs, which provide an index of the plant communities growing in a particular 30-m cell, effectively delineate distinct vegetation types that are meaningful suitability indicators for MPB-caused tree mortality. Our analyses suggested that available geospatial vegetation datasets derived from field data and remotely sensed imagery are useful for producing spatially explicit measures of pine density for use in landscape-level modeling of MPB dynamics.

Keywords: mountain pine beetle, pine density maps, aerial detection survey, LANDFIRE

Authors

Benjamin A. Crabb, Remote Sensing and Geographic Information Systems Laboratory, Department of Wildland Resources, Utah State University, Logan.

James A. Powell, Department of Mathematics and Statistics, Utah State University, Logan.

Barbara J. Bentz, USDA Forest Service, Rocky Mountain Research Station, Logan, Utah.

Contents

Development and Assessment of 30-Meter Pine Density Maps for Landscape-Level Modeling of Mountain Pine Beetle Dynamics

Benjamin A. Crabb, James A. Powell, and Barbara J. Bentz

Introduction

A classic issue in landscape ecology is the prediction of current and future distributions of plant and animal species at spatially relevant scales (Pearson and Dawson 2003; Wiens 1989). Most species are adapted to particular environmental circumstances that define a range of conditions necessary for growth and reproduction (Bentz and others 2011; Savolainen and others 2007). An understanding of species adaptations to environmental conditions can inform the development of spatially explicit species distribution maps. Forecasting species success across a landscape and the landscape's ultimate geographic distribution can be accomplished using mechanistic models (e.g., Kearney and Porter 2009), through statistical association of observed patterns (Guisan and Thuiller 2005), or using some combination of the two. Spatially explicit predictions for insect species that feed on plants will require spatially explicit information on the distribution of host-plant species.

The mountain pine beetle (*Dendroctonus ponderosae* Hopkins [Coleoptera: Curculionidae, Scolytinae], MPB) is an eruptive bark beetle species with significant ecological and economical impact on forest resources (Bentz and others 2010; Safranyik and others 2010). MPB has adapted to feed and reproduce in all *Pinus* species that occur within its current geographic distribution in western North America (Wood 1982). The beetle's strategy for colonizing its well-defended host trees is to synchronize attacks over both time and space, overwhelming host defenses at scales as small as individual trees and small stands of trees. Models for describing and predicting MPB population dynamics vary, ranging from theoretical descriptions of population growth with varying levels of complexity (Berryman and others 1984; Lewis and others 2010) to models that explicitly describe biological processes of MPB attack and reproduction (Powell and others 1996; White and Powell 1997), and to quantitative descriptions of MPB phenology (Bentz and others 1991; Logan and Bentz 1999). A mechanistic, demographic model for MPB was recently developed that builds on previous knowledge and incorporates the important role of phenological synchronization in time for overwhelming host tree defenses and successful reproduction (Powell and Bentz 2009). The model is not spatially explicit, however, at least in part because accurate, spatially explicit host tree density information does not exist on a sufficiently fine scale to drive a mechanistic model. However, forecasting MPB population success and the spatial pattern of that success is an important consideration in forest management. The goal of this study was to develop and evaluate moderate-scale (30-m) host tree density data that can be used to drive a next-generation, spatially explicit model of MPB-caused tree mortality.

Aerial detection surveys (ADS) are annual surveys conducted by USDA Forest Health Protection (FHP) whereby acres impacted (i.e., polygons) by a variety of insect and disease species, including MPB, are estimated and manually drawn on forest maps. MPB impact is discerned as tree mortality, identified as changes in foliage color from green to red as a tree dies. In most parts of the western United States, this change in foliage color occurs over a single year, and there is a one-year lag between MPB host tree colonization and aerial detection of tree mortality. Although ADS provide an annual estimate of pines per hectare killed by MPB, and hence a spatially referenced estimation of MPB population size, they do not provide any measure of prior host pine tree availability. In the topographically complex landscape of the western United States where MPB resides, environmental conditions and host tree distribution can differ at 30-m scales. A spatially explicit database of tree species information at this resolution would be ideal for use with our demographic model to make predictions of MPB population success across large landscapes. Moderate-scale (i.e., 30 m), spatially explicit data of coniferous tree species are not available for all areas of the western United States. However, a number of landscape-scale vegetation datasets at resolutions of 30 m and 250 m contain varying information on plant community groups, in addition to data on tree size and density classes. These vegetation data were derived using satellite imagery and ground plot information (Blackard 2009; Blackard and others 2008; Pierce and others 2009; Ruefenacht and others 2008; USGS 2009).

To develop a spatially explicit database of pine density at 30-m resolution, we used five vegetation datasets derived from satellite imagery and ground plot information, at resolutions of 250 m and 30 m that contain measures of conifer species groups, tree size, and tree density (Blackard 2009; Blackard and others 2008; Pierce and others 2009; Ruefenacht and others 2008; USGS 2009). Additional datasets (Krist and others 2007) were considered but not used due to their more coarse resolution (1 km). We coupled the information taken at 250 m and 30 m resolution with spatially explicit data describing ecologically relevant cover types (USGS 2009) to downscale pine density data to a 30-m scale. We compared results from our approach with an independent prediction of pine host species presence across landscapes derived from ADS data of MPB-caused pine mortality. We acknowledge that ADS data are a relatively coarse estimate of pine mortality caused by MPB. They are, however, the only temporal and spatial data available on MPB population presence across landscapes that can be used in the development and evaluation of MPB models. Three study areas in the western United States with ongoing or recent MPB population outbreaks were chosen to test the methodology: (1) Sawtooth National Recreation Area, Sawtooth National Forest, Idaho; (2) Okanogan-Wenatchee National Forest, Washington; and (3) Medicine Bow-Routt, and Arapaho-Roosevelt National Forests, Colorado and Wyoming. We describe how existing spatial vegetation datasets may be used to develop maps of MPB host tree availability at 30-m resolution for the three study areas.

Methods

Study Areas

We chose three study areas (fig. 1) with ongoing or recent MPB population activity across the northern, central, and southern Rocky Mountain ecoprovinces. The Chelan study area in the northern Rockies encompasses over 446,000 ha, from approximately 47°56'N to 48°35'N and from 119°52'W to 120°44'W. Elevations range from 238 m in the southeast corner, to 336 m at Lake Chelan, and to 2716 m. The study area is comprised of public and private lands, including portions of the Methow Valley and Chelan Ranger Districts, Okanogan-Wenatchee National Forest, and North Cascades National Park. The Methow River drainage characterizes the eastern half of the study area. Coniferous vegetation within the study area include ponderosa (*Pinus ponderosa*), lodgepole (*P. contorta*) and whitebark (*P. albicaulis*) pines; Engelmann spruce (*Picea englemannii*); and Douglas-fir (*Pseudotsugae menziesii*). The Chelan study area boundary was chosen to encompass pine vegetation susceptible to MPB infestation and also included stands where MPB phenology was being monitored (Bentz and Powell, unpublished data).

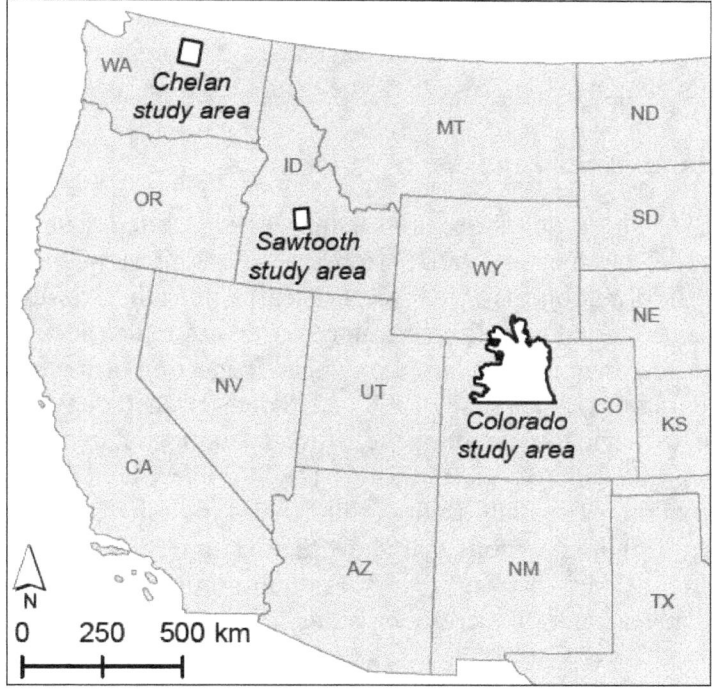

Figure 1. Location of study areas within the western United States.

The Sawtooth study area encompasses over 268,000 ha in central Idaho, from approximately 44°22'N to 43°44'N and 115°10'W to 114°28'W. The landscape is characterized by the Sawtooth Valley and the surrounding mountains, nearly all of which are administered by the Sawtooth National Recreation Area, Sawtooth National Forest. The Challis National Forest covers a northern portion of the study area. Elevation ranges from 1651 m to 3605 m, and vegetation types range from shrub and grasslands to coniferous forests dominated by Douglas-fir, subalpine fir (*Abies lasiocarpa*), lodgepole, and whitebark pines. Extensive barren areas exist above tree-line at the highest elevations. The climate is characterized by very cold winters and mild summers. Extensive studies on MPB phenology and life history have been conducted within the study area boundary (Bentz 2006; Bentz and Mullins 1999; Powell and Bentz 2009).

The Colorado study area is significantly larger than the other two study areas, encompassing over 4,380,000 ha in northern Colorado and southern Wyoming. The study area reaches in the north to approximately 41°50'N, in the east to 105°0'W, and in the west to 108°0'W encompassing portions of the Medicine Bow-Routt and Arapaho-Roosevelt National Forests. Coniferous vegetation includes lodgepole pine, limber pine (*P. flexilis*), Engelmann spruce, subalpine fir, and Douglas-fir. The northern, eastern, and western boundaries are delineated by Multi-Resolution Land Characteristics (MRLC) consortium Zone 28, "Southern Rocky Mountains," (Homer and Gallant 2001) and on the south at approximately 39°10'N. We chose this boundary instead of a rectangular area such as the other two study areas because the contour of U.S. Geological Survey (USGS) Zone 28 captures the vast majority of the MPB impact, and all of our vegetation datasets for the Colorado study area were developed using Zone 28 as the extent for training modeling processes.

Aerial Detection Survey Data

In many USDA Forest Service regions in the western United States, FHP conducts annual aerial detection surveys (ADS) from fixed-wing aircraft. The surveys provide annual trend information on forest insects, diseases, and other causes of tree mortality and damage. During ADS flights, trained observers collect and manually record data on a geo-referenced map based on visual inspection of forest structure, tree species, and foliage color (Halsey 1998). ADS datasets include "damage" polygon shapefiles with metadata describing the estimated number of trees per acre affected and a code for the damage causal agent(s) (DCA). These data serve as our source of information on the spatial location, timing, and intensity of MPB impact. Also included are "flown" polygons that show the extent of area surveyed by the annual ADS flight. These data suggest that not all portions of the study areas were surveyed each year, and we therefore assume some annual MPB was not recorded.

Geo-referenced ADS data is available through the 2010 survey for all study areas (www.foresthealth.info/portal). The first years of available ADS data are 1980, 1991, and 1994 for the Chelan, Sawtooth, and Colorado study areas, respectively. Polygons depicting MPB impact were queried using their unique DCA code by host tree species. For the Colorado study area, we also queried polygons classified under the DCA code for "five-needle pine decline," a code used to describe recent MPB-caused mortality, in association with white pine blister rust, of several five-needle white pine species that grow at high elevations. There were no polygons with the "five-needle pine decline" code in the Sawtooth or Chelan study areas. Raster layers of total MPB impact by year were created by summing MPB impacts across observations for each polygon, which were then converted to rasters. The rasters were produced at a 30-m resolution and were kept in the same coordinate system as the original ADS shapefiles provided by FHP: North American Datum (NAD) 1983 Albers for the Sawtooth and Chelan areas, and NAD 1983 Universal Transverse Mercator (UTM) Zone 13N for the Colorado study area. All other geospatial raster data used in this study were converted into these projections at 30-m resolution using ArcGIS 9.3 software (ESRI 2008).

Vegetation Data

LANDFIRE Existing Vegetation Type (EVT) (30 m)

The inter-agency Landscape Fire and Resource Management Planning Tools Project (LANDFIRE) is a collaborative mapping effort of the USDA Forest Service, Department of the Interior, and The Nature Conservancy (www.landfire.gov; USGS 2009). Nationwide spatial datasets at 30-m resolution have been produced for fire management applications and include layers describing vegetation composition and structure. LANDFIRE vegetation layers include potential and existing vegetation that are predicted using classification and regression trees (www.rulequest.com), extensive field-referenced data (including USDA Forest Service Forest Inventory and Analysis [FIA] plot data), spectral values from Landsat satellite imagery, and biophysical gradient layers. The EVT layer represents the vegetation present at a given site, relative to ground conditions on the date of the most recent remotely sensed imagery used (2002 for our three study areas). EVTs are based on NatureServe's *ecological systems* classification, a nationally consistent set of mid-scale ecological units (Comer and others 2003). EVTs are mapped within zones delineated by the MRLC consortium (Homer and Gallant 2001). Measurements of "agreement" on individual 30-m pixels between LANDFIRE EVT data and other landscape classifications were found to vary from 40-64% in the western United States (http://www.landfire.gov/dp_quality_assessment.php). A recent addition to LANDFIRE is a national tree-list layer (Drury and Herynk 2011). For our study, LANDFIRE EVT data were retained at a 30-m resolution and converted to the coordinate system of ADS shapefiles for each study area.

Conterminous United States (CONUS) Biomass, Forest Type, and Forest Type Groups (250 m)

Geospatial datasets and maps (250-m resolution) of forest biomass (Blackard and others 2008), forest type, and forest type groups (Ruefenacht and others 2008) have been developed for the conterminous United States (CONUS), Alaska, and Puerto Rico by integrating satellite image-based maps of forest land cover and plot data from the FIA program. The CONUS biomass dataset includes estimates of aboveground live forest biomass and was developed using a two step hierarchical process involving two response variables from FIA plot data collected between 1990 and 2003: a binary forest/nonforest mask, and aboveground live forest biomass. Classification trees were used to build the forest/nonforest mask across 65 ecologically unique mapping zones (Homer and Gallant 2001). FIA defines *forest land* as at least 0.405 ha in size, with a minimum continuous canopy width of 36.58 m with at least 10% stocking, and an understory undisturbed by a nonforest land use (such as residences or agriculture) (FIA 2004). Regression trees were then used to model aboveground live forest biomass from those FIA plots found within the predicted forest portion of the mask. *Aboveground live biomass* includes biomass in live tree boles, stumps, branches, and twigs of trees of at least 2.54 cm (1 inch) diameter at breast height (DBH). Biomass values are derived from region- or species-specific allometric equations (Blackard and others 2008). Predictor variables included land cover estimates from 2001 Moderate Resolution Imaging Spectroradiometer (MODIS) imagery, National Land Cover Database (NLCD) classes (Vogelmann and others 2001), climate data, and topographic variables. The current CONUS Biomass dataset refers to a ground condition date of 2001, the date of the MODIS imagery used.

CONUS forest type and forest type groups were also produced using classification trees. The forest/nonforest mask developed by Blackard and others (2008) was initially used to exclude nonforest areas. Forest types and forest type groups were then assigned using response variables collected on FIA plots from pre-1990 to 2004, 55% of which were collected from 2000-2004 (Ruefenacht and others 2008). Forest types were defined using a modified version of Eyre's (1980) classification scheme in which forest types are named after predominate tree species (Ruefenacht and others 2008). Predominance is determined by basal area, and the name of the forest type is usually confined to one or two species (Eyre 1980). Forest types are aggregations of pure stands of forest trees; forest type groups are aggregations of similar forest types. Predictor variables included 2001 MODIS imagery, NLCD classes, and a suite of topographical and gradient datasets. The CONUS dataset includes 141 forest types and 28 forest type groups across the contiguous United States and Alaska (Ruefenacht and others 2008). The current CONUS forest type and forest type group dataset refers to a ground condition date of 2001, the date of the MODIS imagery used. All CONUS data, including biomass, forest type, and forest type groups, were converted to the coordinate system of ADS shapefiles for each study area. The data were resampled to a 30-m resolution using bilinear interpolation for continuous data and nearest neighbor interpolation for categorical data using ArcGIS 9.3 software (ESRI 2008).

Interior West Forest Attributes (250 m)

A dataset of forest attributes (250-m resolution) was developed for the Interior West (IW) FIA region, using a similar approach as previously described for the CONUS datasets (Blackard, IW-FIA Predicted Forest Attribute Maps-2005, 2009) (Blackard and others 2008). Classification and regression trees were used with MODIS imagery (2001-2003), climate, and topographic variables to model several response variables from FIA plot data, including: trees per acre (≥2.54 cm DBH) (TPA), stand density index (≥2.54 cm DBH) (SDI), biomass, forest types, and forest type groups. IW datasets are only available for the Sawtooth and Colorado study areas, and refer to a ground condition date of approximately 2003 (J. Blackard, pers. comm.). The IW data were converted to the coordinate system of ADS shapefiles for each study area (see above) at a 30-m resolution using bilinear interpolation for layers with continuous values and nearest neighbor interpolation for layers with categorical values (ESRI 2008).

GNNFire Project Forest Attributes (30 m)

The GNNFire project (LEMMA 2005; Pierce and others 2009) (hereafter referred to as GNN) developed spatially explicit datasets of forest vegetation and fuels in three ecoregions of the western United States and was based on the Gradient Nearest Neighbor (GNN) method. The Chelan study area is included in this database but not the Sawtooth or all parts of the Colorado study areas. The GNN method imputes to each unsampled map pixel a suite of detailed tree and forest attributes taken from a field inventory plot that has the most similar spectral and environmental characteristics (Ohmann and Gregory 2002). Forest inventory plot data were collected by USDA Forest Service Current Vegetation Survey (CVS), FIA in Eastern Washington (FIAEW), and North Cascades National Park (sampled from 1991-2000). Spectral characteristics were derived from Landsat imagery collected in 1992 and 2000. Other spatial data described environmental gradients, including climate, topography, and disturbance. A nonforest mask derived from the 1992 NLCD (Vogelmann and others 2001) excluded nonforested areas from analysis. Attributes imputed to each 30-m pixel include: basal area of live trees by species (≥2.54 cm DBH), quadratic mean diameter (QMD) of live trees by species (≥2.54 cm DBH), and number of live trees per hectare by species (≥25 cm DBH).

The GNN project produced four map products designed to optimize different mapping objectives ranging from species composition to forest structure. Briefly, the map products produced were: (1) a species model, emphasizing species composition, developed without Landsat imagery; (2) a species-size model, a hybrid between the species and structure models, developed using median-filtered Landsat imagery (median filtering moves a 9-pixel window across the image and assigns the median value to the center pixel) to reduce fine-scale heterogeniety; (3) a structure model, filtered, emphasizing forest structure and developed using median-filtered Landsat imagery; (4) a structure model, unfiltered, the same as (3) but developed using unfiltered satellite imagery.

Estimating Total Tree Density, Proportion Pine, and Pine Density

Our goal was to estimate pine density at a 30-m resolution across the three study areas. We did this by combining relatively coarse resolution (250 m) CONUS and IW datasets with the high resolution (30 m) data of mid-scale ecological units represented by LANDFIRE EVTs to produce estimates of live biomass per hectare (BMS), trees per hectare (TPH), and stand density index (SDI). TPH and SDI are direct estimates of tree density derived from field plot data. Trees per hectare is the number of trees per unit area, and SDI is a measure of relative stand density that incorporates tree size and is independent of stand age and site quality

(Reineke 1933). The methodology has three sequential steps: overall density estimation, proportion pine estimation, and pine density estimation (fig. 2). It was applied in all three study areas using the CONUS and LANDFIRE datasets, and in the Sawtooth and Colorado study areas using the IW and LANDFIRE datasets. In the Chelan study area, additional estimates of overall density and pine density were developed using the four GNN map products.

CONUS and IW-Derived Estimates

In the CONUS dataset, the only explicit measure of vegetation density was tons of aboveground live biomass per hectare (CONUS-BMS). In the IW dataset, explicit measures of tree density include the total number of trees per hectare ≥2.54 cm DBH (IW-TPH), SDI (IW-SDI), and aboveground live biomass (IW-BMS). The IW-SDI layer was calculated using the SDI summation method whereby SDI was calculated for trees by diameter size class, then summed to estimate total stand density (Long 1995). This SDI calculation method has been found to overestimate the density of small trees in uneven-aged stands (Woodall and others 2003). CONUS-BMS, IW-TPA, IW-SDI, and IW-BMS values were only available for those portions of the three study areas classified as forested in the respective CONUS or IW forest/nonforest masks (Blackard 2009; Blackard and others 2008).

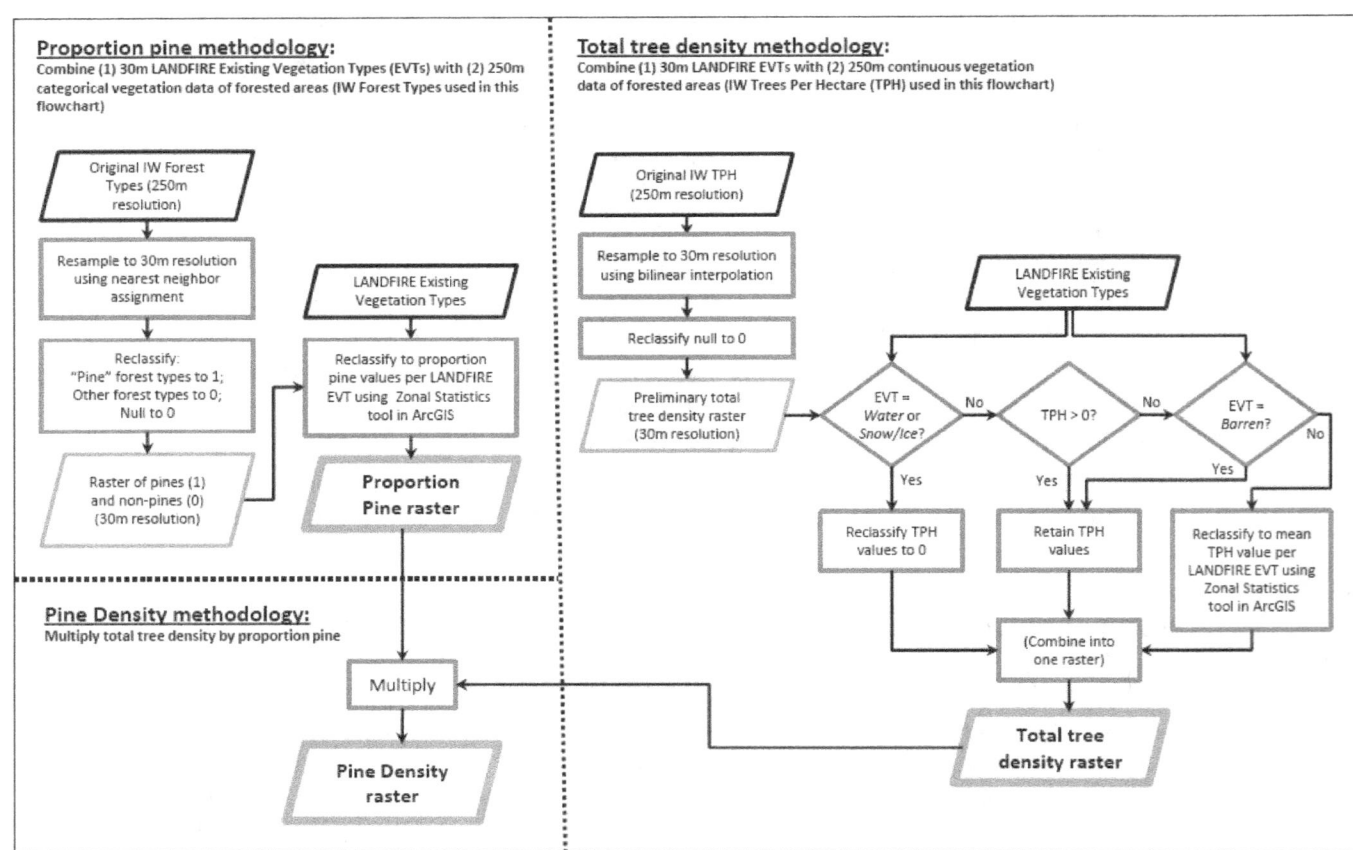

Figure 2. Methodology for developing proportion pine, pine, and total tree density and biomass estimates using 250-m resolution vegetation datasets (see table 1) and 30-m LANDFIRE EVT data.

Nonforested areas identified in the masks could contain at least some proportion forested area. To assign data to these areas at a 30-m resolution LANDFIRE EVT data were used. All CONUS-BMS, IW-TPA, IW-SDI, and IW-BMS nonforest lands were reclassified from null to values of zero tree density. The resulting raster layers were compared against LANDFIRE EVTs to produce a mean tree density statistic for each EVT. Nonforest lands were then reclassified to the mean tree density of the overlapping EVT class in each study area. To correct misclassifications introduced by resampling from 250-m resolution to 30-m resolution, we assigned EVTs *Water* and *Snow/Ice* values of zero tree density. The non-vegetated EVT *Barren* values were assigned zero tree density in those areas also classified as nonforest in the original CONUS or IW data. While this might seem to only adjust landscape densities of trees upwards, it should be noted that the converse process (averaging in portions of EVTs that fall in nonforested lands) adjusts densities downward with equal likelihood. The result was an estimate of overall tree density for the three study areas (right side of fig. 2).

Pine density was calculated using estimates of the overall tree density (described above) and tree species information from the CONUS Forest Type (CONUS-FTP), CONUS Forest Type Group (CONUS-FGP), IW Forest Type (IW-FTP), IW Forest Type Group (IW-FGP), and LANDFIRE EVT data. LANDFIRE EVT classes are at a broader taxonomic scale than the CONUS and IW forest types and forest type group datasets; we therefore used the CONUS-FTP, CONUS-FGP, IW-FTP, and IW-FGP datasets to assign a proportion pine value to each LANDFIRE EVT class. Each dataset was converted to 30-m resolution if necessary. If the FTP or FGP class had pine in the class name, we assumed that pixel was comprised of a majority pine species. Otherwise, the pixel was assumed to have no or very little pine component. For example, IW-FTP pixels classified as "Ponderosa Pine" forest type were re-classified as pine (1), whereas areas classified as "Douglas-Fir" were re-classified as no pine (0). We acknowledge that a FTP or FGP with pine in the title is not necessarily 100% pine, and FTP or FGPs with no pine in the title may also contain some small amount of pine. In the absence of more detailed information, however, we assume that proportions assessed by cross-tabulating the intersection of EVT classes with pine/nonpine FTP or FGP pixels reflect actual proportions within classes. The re-classified pixel values of pine (1) or no pine (0) were overlaid with LANDFIRE EVT pixels, and the proportion of each LANDFIRE EVT class associated with pine pixels was calculated using the Zonal Statistics tool in ArcGIS 9.3. For example, if 15% of the EVT Northern Rocky Mountain Mesic Montane Mixed Conifer Forest pixels were associated with IW-FTP pine pixels, we assumed that EVT pixels with a Northern Rocky Mountain Mesic Montane Mixed Conifer Forest class contained 15% pine. Pine density estimates for each pixel were produced by multiplying a measure of overall tree density (derived from CONUS-BMS, IW-SDI, IW-TPH, or IW-BMS) by a measure of proportion pine (derived from CONUS-FTP, CONUS-FGP, IW-FTP, or IW-FGP; bottom of fig. 2). Unique pine density estimates were produced by combining the CONUS-derived overall density estimate (CONUS-BMS) with each CONUS-derived proportion pine estimate (from CONUS-FTP and CONUS-FGP), and by combining each IW-derived overall density estimate (IW-TPH, IW-SDI, and IW-BMS) with each

IW-derived proportion pine estimate (from IW-FTP and IW- FGP). This produced two pine density estimates for all three study areas (CONUS-BMS-FTP and CONUS-BMS-FGP) and six additional pine density estimates for the Sawtooth and Colorado study areas (IW-SDI-FTP, IW-SDI-FGP, IW-TPH-FTP, IW-TPH-FGP, IW-BMS-FTP, and IW-BMS-FGP)

Chelan Study Area

In addition to pine density estimates from CONUS-BMS-FTP and CONUS-BMS-FGP, the four GNN map products were used to produce additional overall density and pine density estimates for the Chelan study area. Pixels in the GNN map products are linked to a tabular database of detailed plot-level forest attribute information based on that pixel's nearest neighbor in gradient space. A pixel's associated nearest neighboring plot can vary among the four maps based on the objectives emphasized in the GNN modeling process (e.g., species composition versus forest structure [described above]), resulting in differing maps of forest attributes. To produce overall density estimates and pine density estimates from the four GNN models, we manipulated the tabular database and attached the results to each of the GNN maps using ArcGIS 9.3.

Tabular GNN data have explicit measurements of tree density in addition to basal area measurements for up to 31 tree species per plot. For each plot, we calculated the proportion of total basal area represented by the four pine species in the GNN database (whitebark pine, lodgepole pine, western white pine, and ponderosa pine). These proportion pine estimates were attached to the GNN models and exported to raster datasets across the Chelan study area. Measures of tree density available in the GNN dataset, trees per hectare (GNN-TPH), conifer trees per hectare (GNN-CTPH), and stand density index (GNN-SDI), were used to estimate overall tree and pine-only density values for each plot. TPH and CTPH were available across six size classes: (1) ≥2.54 cm DBH, (2) 2.54-25 cm DBH, (3) 25-50 cm DBH, (4) 50-75 cm DBH, (5) 75-100 cm DBH, and (6) ≥100 cm DBH. TPH and SDI were attached to each GNN model in a GIS, and plot-level values were exported as raster layers. A measure of pine SDI (GNN-PSDI) was calculated by multiplying the plot-level SDI values with the proportion of all basal area that was pine in that plot. To convert CTPH to the number of pine trees per hectare (GNN-PTPH), the proportion of all conifer basal area that was pine in each plot was calculated and then multiplied by CTPH for each size class. The GNN-PTPH values were then attached to the GNN models and exported to raster datasets across the Chelan study area resulting in pine TPH (GNN-PTPH) for the six size classes.

Assessing Tree Density and Proportion Pine Estimates Using ADS and Landfire EVT Classes

Using variables of tree density and tree species from several vegetation datasets (i.e., CONUS, IW, and GNN), we estimated total tree density and biomass, and pine density and biomass across the three study areas at a final resolution of 30 m (table 1). Also available for each 30-m pixel was a measure of MPB impact (trees killed/ha) derived from annual ADS for each study area. If we assume that MPB impacts (trees/ha) are higher where there is a greater proportion pine and/or a greater density of pines, the main tree species attacked by MPB, then we can use the ADS data (TPH pine affected by MPB) to evaluate our proportion pine and pine and total tree density measurements derived from the independent vegetation datasets. To do this, we used LANDFIRE EVTs as the units of analysis. Predictor variables were produced by cross-tabulating the matrix of estimated vegetation values with LANDFIRE pixels and EVT values to produce estimates for each study area of average biomass, total tree density, and pine density by LANDFIRE EVT class. The response variable was average cumulative MPB impact (pine trees killed per ha) per EVT, total number of pines killed over all years of available ADS divided by total hectares covered by each EVT.

Table 1. Geospatial vegetation datasets used to model estimates of pine and total tree density and biomass and proportion pine for three study areas: Sawtooth, Chelan, and Colorado. All estimates for the Sawtooth and Colorado study areas used the LANDFIRE EVT dataset[a] in conjunction with the listed vegetation dataset, following the methodology shown in fig. 2.

Models of proportion pine			
Vegetation model	**Units**	**Vegetation dataset**	**Study area**
IW-FTP-PP	None	IW Forest Types[b]	Sawtooth, Colorado
IW-FGP-PP	None	IW Forest Type Groups[b]	Sawtooth, Colorado
CONUS-FTP-PP	None	CONUS Forest Types[c]	Sawtooth, Colorado, Chelan
CONUS-FGP-PP	None	CONUS Forest Type Groups[c]	Sawtooth, Colorado, Chelan
GNN-SP-PP	None	GNN species model[d]	Chelan
GNN-SZ-PP	None	GNN species-size model[d]	Chelan
GNN-SF-PP	None	GNN structure (filtered) model[d]	Chelan
GNN-SU-PP	None	GNN structure (unfiltered) model[d]	Chelan
Models of total tree density			
Vegetation model	**Units**	**Source data**	**Study area**
IW-SDI	Trees/ha, stand Quadratic Mean Diameter (QMD) forced to 25 cm	IW Stand Density Index[b] (SDI)	Sawtooth, Colorado
IW-TPH	Trees/ha of ≥2.54 cm DBH	IW Trees Per Hectare[b] (TPH)	Sawtooth, Colorado
IW-BMS	Tons of aboveground live biomass/ha	IW Biomass[b]	Sawtooth, Colorado
CONUS-BMS	Tons of aboveground live biomass/ha	CONUS Biomass[e]	Sawtooth, Colorado, Chelan
GNN-SP-SDI GNN-SZ-SDI GNN-SF-SDI GNN-SU-SDI	Trees/ha, given stand QMD forced to 25 cm	GNN species model[d] GNN species-size model[d] GNN structure (filtered) model[d] GNN structure (unfiltered) model[d]	Chelan
GNN-SP-TPH-GE3 GNN-SZ-TPH-GE3 GNN-SF-TPH-GE3 GNN-SU-TPH-GE3	Trees/ha of ≥2.54 cm DBH	GNN species model[d] GNN species-size model[d] GNN structure (filtered) model[d] GNN structure (unfiltered) model[d]	Chelan

Table 1. Continued).

Models of total tree density			
Vegetation model	**Units**	**Source data**	**Study area**
GNN-SP-TPH-3-25 GNN-SZ-TPH-3-25 GNN-SF-TPH-3-25 GNN-SU-TPH-3-25	Trees/ha of 2.54-25 cm DBH	GNN species model[d] GNN species-size model[d] GNN structure (filtered) model[d] GNN structure (unfiltered) model[d]	Chelan
GNN-SP-TPH-25-50 GNN-SZ-TPH-25-50 GNN-SF-TPH-25-50 GNN-SU-TPH-25-50	Trees/ha of 25-50 cm DBH	GNN species model[d] GNN species-size model[d] GNN structure (filtered) model[d] GNN structure (unfiltered) model[d]	Chelan
GNN-SP-TPH-50-75 GNN-SZ-TPH-50-75 GNN-SF-TPH-50-75 GNN-SU-TPH-50-75	Trees/ha of 50-75 cm DBH	GNN species model[d] GNN species-size model[d] GNN structure (filtered) model[d] GNN structure (unfiltered) model[d]	Chelan
GNN-SP-TPH-75-100 GNN-SZ-TPH-75-100 GNN-SF-TPH-75-100 GNN-SU-TPH-75-100	Trees/ha of 75-100 cm DBH	GNN species model[d] GNN species-size model[d] GNN structure (filtered) model[d] GNN structure (unfiltered) model[d]	Chelan
GNN-SP-TPH-GE100 GNN-SZ-TPH-GE100 GNN-SF-TPH-GE100 GNN-SU-TPH-GE100	Trees/ha of ≥100 cm DBH	GNN species model[d] GNN species-size model[d] GNN structure (filtered) model[d] GNN structure (unfiltered) model[d]	Chelan
Models of pine tree density			
Vegetation model	**Units**	**Source data**	**Study area**
IW-SDI-FTP	*Pinus* trees/ha, given stand QMD forced to 25 cm	IW SDI and IW Forest Types[b]	Sawtooth, Colorado
IW-SDI-FGP	*Pinus* trees/ha, given stand QMD forced to 25 cm	IW SDI and IW Forest Type Groups[b]	Sawtooth, Colorado
IW-TPH-FTP	*Pinus* trees/ha of ≥2.54 cm DBH	IW TPA and IW Forest Types[b]	Sawtooth, Colorado
IW-TPH-FGP	*Pinus* trees/ha of ≥2.54 cm DBH	IW TPA and IW Forest Type Groups[b]	Sawtooth, Colorado
IW-BMS-FTP	Tons of aboveground live *Pinus* biomass/ha	IW Biomass & IW Forest Types[b]	Sawtooth, Colorado
IW-BMS-FGP	Tons of aboveground live *Pinus* biomass/ha	IW Biomass & IW Forest Type Groups[b]	Sawtooth, Colorado
CONUS-BMS-FTP	Tons of aboveground live *Pinus* biomass/ha	CONUS Biomass[e] & CONUS Forest Types[c]	Sawtooth, Colorado, Chelan
CONUS-BMS-FGP	Tons of aboveground live *Pinus* biomass/ha	CONUS Biomass[e] & CONUS Forest Type Groups[c]	Sawtooth, Colorado, Chelan
GNN-SP-PSDI GNN-SZ-PSDI GNN-SF-PSDI GNN-SU-PSDI	*Pinus* trees/ha, given stand QMD forced to 25 cm	GNN species model[d] GNN species-size model[d] GNN structure (filtered) model[d] GNN structure (unfiltered) model[d]	Chelan

Table 1. Continued).

Models of pine tree density			
Vegetation model	**Units**	**Source data**	**Study area**
GNN-SP-PTPH-GE3 GNN-SZ-PTPH-GE3 GNN-SF-PTPH-GE3 GNN-SU-PTPH-GE3	*Pinus* trees/ha of ≥2.54 cm DBH	GNN species model[d] GNN species-size model[d] GNN structure (filtered) model[d] GNN structure (unfiltered) model[d]	Chelan
GNN-SP-PTPH-3-25 GNN-SZ-PTPH-3-25 GNN-SF-PTPH-3-25 GNN-SU-PTPH-3-25	*Pinus* trees/ha of 2.54-25 cm DBH	GNN species model[d] GNN species-size model[d] GNN structure (filtered) model[d] GNN structure (unfiltered) model[d]	Chelan
GNN-SP-PTPH-25-50 GNN-SZ-PTPH-25-50 GNN-SF-PTPH-25-50 GNN-SU-PTPH-25-50	*Pinus* trees/ha of 25-50 cm DBH	GNN species model[d] GNN species-size model[d] GNN structure (filtered) model[d] GNN structure (unfiltered) model[d]	Chelan
GNN-SP-PTPH-50-75 GNN-SZ-PTPH-50-75 GNN-SF-PTPH-50-75 GNN-SU-PTPH-50-75	*Pinus* trees/ha of 50-75 cm DBH	GNN species model[d] GNN species-size model[d] GNN structure (filtered) model[d] GNN structure (unfiltered) model[d]	Chelan
GNN-SP-PTPH-75-100 GNN-SZ-PTPH-75-100 GNN-SF-PTPH-75-100 GNN-SU-PTPH-75-100	*Pinus* trees/ha of 75-100 cm DBH	GNN species model[d] GNN species-size model[d] GNN structure (filtered) model[d] GNN structure (unfiltered) model[d]	Chelan
GNN-SP-PTPH-GE100 GNN-SZ-PTPH-GE100 GNN-SF-PTPH-GE100 GNN-SU-PTPH-GE100	*Pinus* trees/ha of ≥100 cm DBH	GNN species model[d] GNN species-size model[d] GNN structure (filtered) model[d] GNN structure (unfiltered) model[d]	Chelan

[a] USGS 2009
[b] Blackard 2009
[c] Ruefenacht and others 2008
[d] Pierce and others 2009; LEMMA 2010
[e] Blackard and others 2008

Linear regression analyses and negative binomial regression (R Development Core Team 2010) were used to determine the strength of the relationship between cumulative MPB impact and estimates of pine and total tree density, as well as pine and total biomass from the three vegetation datasets (table 1) for each LANDFIRE EVT by study area (table 2). EVTs vary in spatial prevalence (size) and share of total MPB impact across the three study areas. Linear regression provided the best fits in all cases and was used in subsequent analyses. To understand how well our density estimates compared with ADS records of MPB impact in those EVTs that are large or have a large proportion of total MPB impact, both weighted and unweighted regressions were performed for each vegetation model. These included an area-weighted regression in which weights were determined by the total area of each EVT, and a mortality-weighted regression in which weights were determined by the cumulative number of trees killed by MPB in each EVT. Un-weighted regression analysis was also used to assess the utility of EVTs as units of analysis by testing whether the simple spatial prevalence of an EVT predicts the amount of MPB impact it receives.

Table 2. LANDFIRE EVT classes represented in each study area (SA) and used in vegetation analyses. The amount of area covered by each EVT class and proportion of the study area are shown. EVT classes comprising <180 ha in each of the study areas are not shown here.

Class	EVT name	Sawtooth		Colorado		Chelan	
		Hectares	% of SA	Hectares	% of SA	Hectares	% of SA
11	Open Water	2,352	0.88%	30,410	0.69%	10,850	2.43%
12	Snow-Ice	1,079	0.40%	65,342	1.49%	44	0.01%
21	Developed-Open Space	89	0.03%	31,686	0.72%	313	0.07%
22	Developed-Low Intensity	92	0.03%	12,272	0.28%	3,314	0.74%
23	Developed-Medium Intensity	22	0.01%	2,722	0.06%	47	0.01%
24	Developed-High Intensity	0.2	0.00%	270	0.01%	161	0.04%
31	Barren	58,343	21.71%	122,378	2.79%	4,191	0.94%
81	Agriculture-Pasture and Hay	1,271	0.47%	85,133	1.94%	1,449	0.32%
82	Agriculture-Cultivated Crops and Irrigated Agriculture	143	0.05%	102,928	2.35%	4,667	1.04%
83	Agriculture-Small Grains					245	0.05%
2001	Inter-Mountain Basins Sparsely Vegetated Systems	0.6	0.00%	61	0.00%	507	0.11%
2006	Rocky Mountain Alpine/Montane Sparsely Vegetated Systems	17	0.01%	346	0.01%	846	0.19%
2011	Rocky Mountain Aspen Forest and Woodland	12,067	4.49%	386,611	8.82%	196	0.04%
2016	Colorado Plateau Pinyon-Juniper Woodland			83,579	1.91%		
2018	East Cascades Mesic Montane Mixed-Conifer Forest and Woodland					7,267	1.63%
2037	North Pacific Maritime Dry-Mesic Douglas-fir-Western Hemlock Forest					978	0.22%
2038	North Pacific Maritime Mesic Subalpine Parkland					1,136	0.25%
2041	North Pacific Mountain Hemlock Forest					2,419	0.54%
2045	Northern Rocky Mountain Dry-Mesic Montane Mixed Conifer Forest	1,373	0.51%			156,626	35.07%
2046	Northern Rocky Mountain Subalpine Woodland and Parkland	31,464	11.71%	0.3	0.00%	34,076	7.63%
2049	Rocky Mountain Foothill Limber Pine-Juniper Woodland			3,119	0.07%		
2050	Rocky Mountain Lodgepole Pine Forest	8,410	3.13%	619,008	14.12%	5,951	1.33%

(con.)

Table 2. (Continued).

Class	EVT name	Sawtooth		Colorado		Chelan	
		Hectares	% of SA	Hectares	% of SA	Hectares	% of SA
2051	Southern Rocky Mountain Dry-Mesic Montane Mixed Conifer Forest and Woodland			209,569	4.78%		
2052	Southern Rocky Mountain Mesic Montane Mixed Conifer Forest and Woodland			91,058	2.08%		
2053	Northern Rocky Mountain Ponderosa Pine Woodland and Savanna	15	0.01%			17,783	3.98%
2054	Southern Rocky Mountain Ponderosa Pine Woodland			176,176	4.02%		
2055	Rocky Mountain Subalpine Dry-Mesic Spruce-Fir Forest and Woodland	21,105	7.86%	825,177	18.83%	2,042	0.46%
2056	Rocky Mountain Subalpine Mesic-Wet Spruce-Fir Forest and Woodland	4,151	1.55%	24,619	0.56%	21,868	4.90%
2057	Rocky Mountain Subalpine-Montane Limber-Bristlecone Pine Woodland			6,891	0.16%		
2059	Southern Rocky Mountain Pinyon-Juniper Woodland			4,203	0.10%		
2061	Inter-Mountain Basins Aspen-Mixed Conifer Forest and Woodland	134	0.05%	399,821	9.12%		
2062	Inter-Mountain Basins Curl-leaf Mountain Mahogany Woodland and Shrubland			256	0.01%		
2064	Colorado Plateau Mixed Low Sagebrush Shrubland			582	0.01%		
2065	Columbia Plateau Scabland Shrubland					333	0.07%
2068	North Pacific Dry and Mesic Alpine Dwarf-Shrubland or Fell-field or Meadow					1,8133	4.06%
2080	Inter-Mountain Basins Big Sagebrush Shrubland	26	0.01%	374,471	8.54%	4,295	0.96%
2081	Inter-Mountain Basins Mixed Salt Desert Scrub			9,280	0.21%	0.2	0.00%
2083	North Pacific Avalanche Chute Shrubland					5,750	1.29%
2084	North Pacific Montane Shrubland					2,516	0.56%

(con.)

Table 2. (Continued).

Class	EVT name	Sawtooth		Colorado		Chelan	
		Hectares	% of SA	Hectares	% of SA	Hectares	% of SA
2086	Rocky Mountain Lower Montane-Foothill Shrubland			166,286	3.79%		
2093	Southern Colorado Plateau Sand Shrubland			4,858	0.11%		
2106	Northern Rocky Mountain Montane-Foothill Deciduous Shrubland	1,825	0.68%	1	0.00%	8,791	1.97%
2107	Rocky Mountain Gambel Oak-Mixed Montane Shrubland			23,659	0.54%		
2117	Southern Rocky Mountain Ponderosa Pine Savanna			426	0.01%		
2119	Southern Rocky Mountain Juniper Woodland and Savanna			656	0.01%		
2123	Columbia Plateau Steppe and Grassland					2,761	0.62%
2124	Columbia Plateau Low Sagebrush Steppe	1,560	0.58%			103	0.02%
2125	Inter-Mountain Basins Big Sagebrush Steppe	278	0.10%	476	0.01%	3,4200	7.66%
2126	Inter-Mountain Basins Montane Sagebrush Steppe	5,955	2.22%	2423	0.06%	5,967	1.34%
2127	Inter-Mountain Basins Semi-Desert Shrub-Steppe	14	0.01%	1670	0.04%	4	0.00%
2135	Inter-Mountain Basins Semi-Desert Grassland			954	0.02%	33	0.01%
2139	Northern Rocky Mountain Lower Montane-Foothill-Valley Grassland	672	0.25%	46	0.00%	47,888	10.72%
2140	Northern Rocky Mountain Subalpine-Upper Montane Grassland	10,491	3.90%			1	0.00%
2142	Columbia Basin Palouse Prairie					899	0.20%
2143	Rocky Mountain Alpine Fell-Field			308	0.01%		
2144	Rocky Mountain Alpine Turf			71,361	1.63%		
2145	Rocky Mountain Subalpine-Montane Mesic Meadow	262	0.10%	43,152	0.98%		
2146	Southern Rocky Mountain Montane-Subalpine Grassland			34,431	0.79%		
2153	Inter-Mountain Basins Greasewood Flat			540	0.01%		

(con.)

Table 2. (Continued).

Class	EVT name	Sawtooth		Colorado		Chelan	
		Hectares	% of SA	Hectares	% of SA	Hectares	% of SA
2154	Inter-Mountain Basins Montane Riparian Systems	0.8	0.00%	25	0.00%	1,131	0.25%
2156	North Pacific Lowland Riparian Forest and Shrubland					3,390	0.76%
2158	North Pacific Montane Riparian Woodland and Shrubland					4,541	1.02%
2159	Rocky Mountain Montane Riparian Systems	293	0.11%	50,941	1.16%	91	0.02%
2160	Rocky Mountain Subalpine/Upper Montane Riparian Systems	4,466	1.66%	61,447	1.40%		
2161	Northern Rocky Mountain Conifer Swamp	2,037	0.76%				
2165	Northern Rocky Mountain Foothill Conifer Wooded Steppe					965	0.22%
2166	Middle Rocky Mountain Montane Douglas-fir Forest and Woodland	6,010	2.24%				
2167	Rocky Mountain Poor-Site Lodgepole Pine Forest	822	0.31%				
2169	Northern Rocky Mountain Subalpine Deciduous Shrubland	9241	3.44%			2	0.00%
2171	North Pacific Alpine and Subalpine Dry Grassland					16,420	3.68%
2174	North Pacific Dry-Mesic Silver Fir-Western Hemlock-Douglas-fir Forest					5,539	1.24%
2178	North Pacific Hypermaritime Western Red-cedar-Western Hemlock Forest					264	0.06%
2181	Introduced Upland Vegetation-Annual Grassland			785	0.02%	567	0.13%
2182	Introduced Upland Vegetation-Perennial Grassland and Forbland	105	0.04%	24,685	0.56%	1280	0.29%
2186	Introduced Upland Vegetation-Shrub					348	0.08%
2217	Quercus gambelii Shrubland Alliance			162,905	3.72%		
2220	Artemisia tridentata ssp. vaseyana Shrubland Alliance	20903	7.78%	62,247	1.42%	1483	0.33%
2227	Pseudotsuga menziesii Forest Alliance	61,586	22.92%			1344	0.30%
	Total (this table)	268,674	>99.99%	4,382,249	>99.99%	446,016	>99.99%
	Study area total	268,676	100%	4,382,519	100%	446,659	100%

We eliminated EVTs with fewer than 2000 pixels (180 ha) from all regression analyses, reasoning that the small number of coarse-resolution pixels used to compute proportion pine values in these EVTs would be insufficient to produce reliable estimates of proportion pine. In this way, we excluded 16, 16, and 21 EVTs from the Sawtooth, Colorado, and Chelan study areas, respectively, representing 0.25%, 0.01%, and 0.25% of the study areas. The total number of EVTs remaining for model assessment were 25, 47, and 43 in the Sawtooth, Colorado, and Chelan study areas, respectively. EVTs that encompass >180 ha in any of the study areas are shown in Table 2.

Evaluation of LANDFIRE EVTs for Predicting MPB-Caused Pine Mortality

We defined landscape units of analyses based on their LANDFIRE EVT classification, which is an index of the plant communities growing in a particular 30-m cell. Our estimates of pine density (i.e., proportion pine, pine, total tree density, and biomass) were then correlated with MPB impact derived from ADS information using the EVT as the unit of analyses (see above). It is unclear, however, if using the EVT classifications as the unit of analyses, compared to a completely random landscape value with no information on plant communities, increased the correlation between our pine density estimates and MPB impact. To assess if EVTs were meaningful units of analysis for predicting MPB-caused pine mortality, we generated 1000 random landscapes for each study area. In each realization, the number of classes, size (area) of classes, and spatial contiguity of classes approximated that of LANDFIRE EVTs. Using the density estimate (i.e., proportion pine, pine, total tree density, and biomass) that was found to be most correlated with MPB impacts (as assessed using EVTs), we repeated the weighted and un-weighted regression analyses using the randomly generated landscape classes as units of analysis.

Alternate landscape classifications were created from randomly generated points and the natural neighbor interpolation method. Random points were created at an overall density of one point per 10 km^2 across regions defined by the study areas plus a 5-km buffer zone. Each point was at least 1 km from any other point. This process created 382, 589, and 5166 points in the Sawtooth, Chelan, and Colorado study areas, respectively. Each point was then assigned an integer ranging from 1 to n, where n = the number of EVTs in the study area with greater than 2000 pixels. Each integer value had an assignment probability that was equal to the proportion of the study area that was composed by a particular EVT. For example, in the Sawtooth study area, there were 25 EVTs with greater than 2000 pixels, so points in that study area were assigned numbers ranging from 1 to 25. The EVT Rocky Mountain Lodgepole Pine Forest composed 3.13% of the Sawtooth study area, so the integer value associated with this EVT had a 3.13% probability of being assigned to a random point. EVTs that composed large proportions of the study area were assigned integer values closer to n/2; less prevalent EVTs were assigned integer values further from n/2. This was done to ensure that the distribution of size classes in the raster interpolated from these points would approximate the distribution of size classes of the real EVTs.

After all points were assigned values, a surface raster was interpolated across the study area using the natural neighbor method, which interpolates values to query locations using Thiessen polygons. Thiessen polygons are defined around individual sample points so that all locations within the polygon are closer to the point within that polygon than to any other sample point (fig. 3). To interpolate values to unsampled locations, the natural neighbor interpolation technique draws temporary Thiessen polygons around unsampled points and computes the area of overlap with surrounding Thiessen polygons derived from sampled locations. The interpolated value assigned to the unsampled location was then calculated by weighting the values of the surrounding polygons by the area of overlap with the new polygon (fig. 3).

Natural neighbor interpolation creates a continuous surface raster. To classify this continuous raster into categorical zones, we split the raster into n categories using the Slice tool in ArcGIS 9.3 (ESRI 2008). Categories were created by slicing the range of values in the continuous raster into n categories based on equal value intervals. The resulting categories were roughly analogous to LANDFIRE EVTs in two important ways. First, the distribution of sizes of the randomly generated categories approximated the distribution of sizes of the real EVTs. Second, the randomly generated categories were distributed in spatially contiguous patches (that is, the random categories were not defined by the random assignment of each individual cell) (fig. 4). We generated the random landscapes at a 300-m resolution to speed the computing process.

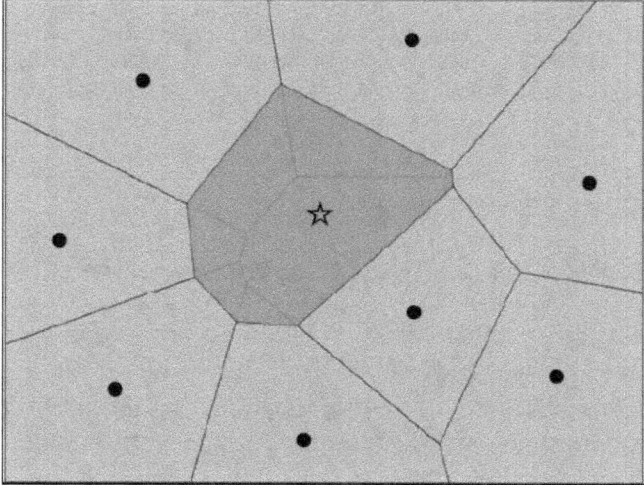

Figure 3. An example of natural neighbor interpolation. The brown polygons are Thiessen polygons defined around sample points (dots). The natural neighbor method interpolates values to unsampled locations, such as the star here, by constructing Thiessen polygons around them (red polygon). Polygons that overlap the new polygon are considered the interpolation point's natural neighbors. The interpolated value is calculated by weighting the values of the surrounding polygons by the area of overlap with the new polygon.

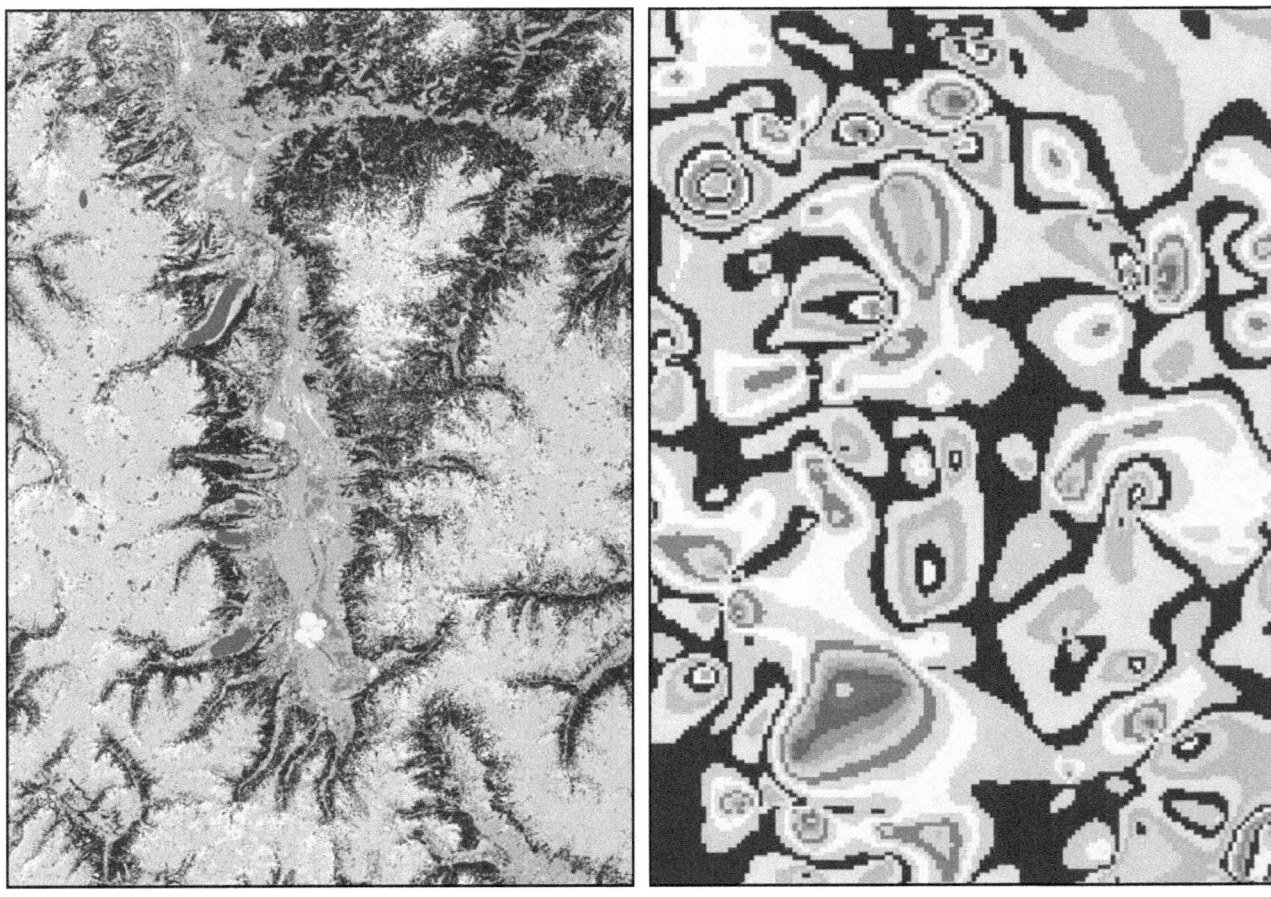

Figure 4. Comparison of the spatial pattern of LANDFIRE EVTs in the Sawtooth study area (left) and an alternate landscape "classification" created from randomly generated points and the natural neighbor interpolation method (right). The prevalence of each class is roughly equal, but the classes on the random landscape do not respect the underlying topography or transition relationships among classes.

Results

Estimates of MPB-Caused Tree Mortality Based on ADS

Annual pine mortality due to MPB was estimated using ADS data for each study area (fig. 5). Because the study areas differ in overall size and ADS were conducted for a different number of years depending on the study area, comparison of overall impact among areas is not valid. In the Sawtooth study area in particular, MPB-caused tree mortality may be underestimated because some areas were not covered by ADS in the early years of the outbreak. Data suggest that MPB population activity peaked in 2007 and 2008 in the Colorado and Chelan study areas, respectively, and that in the Sawtooth study area, MPB-caused tree mortality peaked in the early 2000s and returned to background levels by 2005 (fig. 5). Ideally, the date the vegetation data were collected (i.e., the date of the remotely sensed imagery used in vegetation dataset development) would be prior to the onset of MPB activity at each study area. LANDFIRE is based on an imagery date of 2002, IW is based on 2003, and GNN is based on 2000.

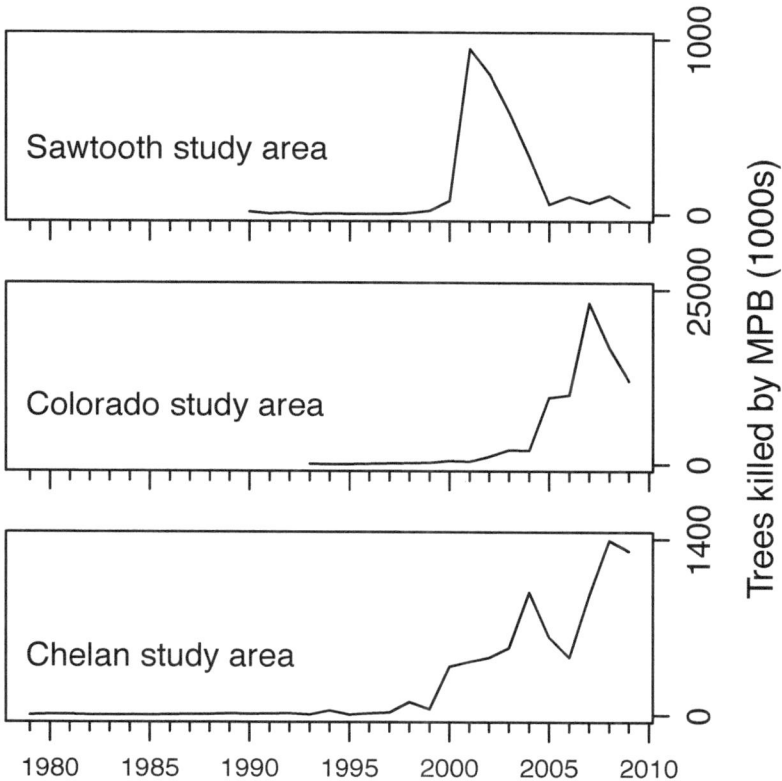

Figure 5. Trees killed by MPB per year by study area based on ADS data. Shown are the years of MPB attack. There is a 1-year lag in ADS data. Peak outbreak years were 2001 in the Sawtooth study area, 2007 in the Colorado study area, and 2008 in the Chelan study area.

These dates are just after MPB activity began in the Chelan and Sawtooth study areas, and before MPB activity in the Colorado study area. We acknowledge this may influence our results. To assess the variable(s) and vegetation dataset(s) that best describe proportion pine and density across the three study areas, we regressed TPH pine affected by MPB (from ADS) with our derived estimates of proportion pine and pine and total tree density (described above) per EVT value. Our main goal was to map MPB host availability, and the most direct measure of MPB host availability is ADS data describing MPB-caused tree mortality (fig. 6). Therefore, mortality-weighted R^2 values were the most informative summary statistics with which to assess our estimates of pine and total tree density and biomass. We report the results of un-weighted, area-weighted, and mortality-weighted regressions in tables 3, 4, 5, 6, and 7 and focus on results from the mortality weighted regressions here.

Pine stem density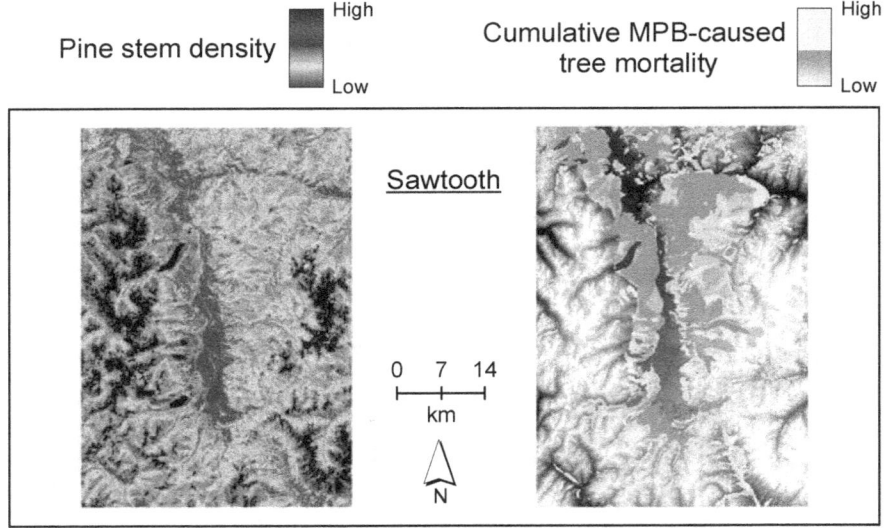

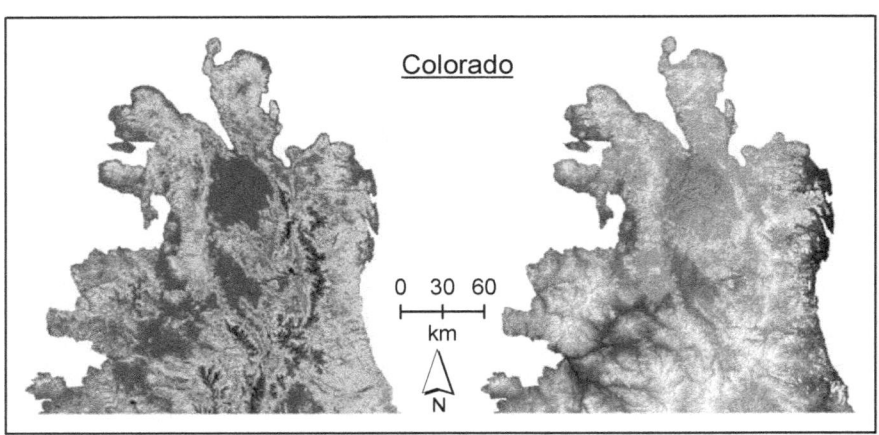

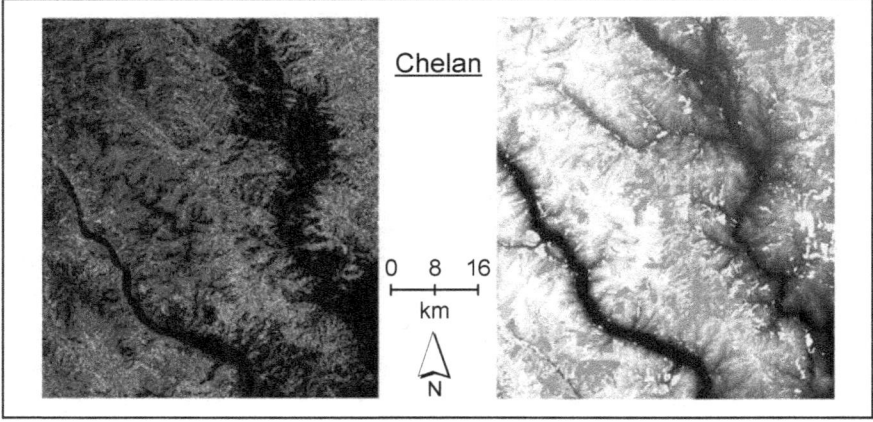

Figure 6. Comparison of pine stem density estimates (TPH) and cumulative MPB-caused tree mortality (TPH killed by MPB). Cumulative MPB-caused tree mortality data are from ADS data collected at the Sawtooth study area from 1991-2010, at the Colorado study area from 1994-2010, and at the Chelan study area from 1980-2010. Regions of highest MPB impact show a relationship with regions of highest pine density, with the exception of Colorado's Front Range (far eastern portion of Colorado maps). To date, the MPB outbreak continues in this area.

Table 3. Regression results for the Sawtooth study area comparing mean cumulative MPB-caused tree mortality (TPH) from ADS and estimates of total biomass (BMS), pine biomass (BMS-FTP and BMS-FGP), total tree density (SDI and TPH) pine density (SDI-FTP, SDI-FGP, TPH-FTP, and TPH-FGP), and proportion pine (FTP-PP and FGP-PP) from two independent vegetation datasets (CONUS and IW). Pine density estimates are in bold. Measures of stem density are shaded. Degrees of freedom in all regressions = 23.

Vegetation variable	Unweighted R^2	p	Area weighted R^2	p	Mortality weighted R^2	p
IW-BMS-FGP	0.941	<0.001	0.926	<0.001	0.926	<0.001
IW-BMS-FTP	0.932	<0.001	0.913	<0.001	0.904	<0.001
IW-SDI-FGP	0.915	<0.001	0.902	<0.001	0.903	<0.001
IW-TPH-FGP	0.925	<0.001	0.892	<0.001	0.897	<0.001
IW-FTP-PP	0.871	<0.001	0.839	<0.001	0.888	<0.001
IW-TPH-FTP	0.916	<0.001	0.881	<0.001	0.876	<0.001
IW-FGP-PP	0.883	<0.001	0.793	<0.001	0.874	<0.001
CONUS-BMS-FGP	0.928	<0.001	0.867	<0.001	0.870	<0.001
IW-SDI-FTP	0.902	<0.001	0.882	<0.001	0.868	<0.001
CONUS-BMS-FTP	0.901	<0.001	0.766	<0.001	0.815	<0.001
CONUS-FGP-PP	0.829	<0.001	0.582	<0.001	0.774	<0.001
CONUS-FTP-PP	0.781	<0.001	0.472	<0.001	0.715	<0.001
CONUS-BMS	0.500	<0.001	0.647	<0.001	0.313	0.004
IW-BMS	0.537	<0.001	0.628	<0.001	0.279	0.007
IW-TPH	0.498	<0.001	0.556	<0.001	0.230	0.015
IW-SDI	0.427	<0.001	0.528	<0.001	0.144	0.061

Table 4. Regression results for the Colorado study area comparing mean cumulative MPB-caused tree mortality (TPH) from ADS and estimates of total biomass (BMS), pine biomass (BMS-FTP and BMS-FGP), total tree density (SDI and TPH), pine density (SDI-FTP, SDI-FGP, TPH-FTP, and TPH-FGP), and proportion pine (FTP-PP and FGP-PP) from two independent vegetation datasets (CONUS and IW). Vegetation variables were estimated for each LANDFIRE EVT value. Pine density estimates are in bold. Measures of stem density are shaded. Degrees of freedom in all regressions = 45.

Vegetation variable	Unweighted R^2	p	Area weighted R^2	p	Mortality weighted R^2	p
CONUS-BMS-FTP	0.806	<0.001	0.899	<0.001	0.950	<0.001
CONUS-BMS-FGP	0.811	<0.001	0.894	<0.001	0.946	<0.001
IW-BMS-FGP	0.810	<0.001	0.889	<0.001	0.944	<0.001
IW-SDI-FGP	0.745	<0.001	0.836	<0.001	0.918	<0.001
IW-BMS-FTP	0.834	<0.001	0.882	<0.001	0.917	<0.001
IW-TPH-FGP	0.714	<0.001	0.812	<0.001	0.905	<0.001
IW-SDI-FTP	0.779	<0.001	0.845	<0.001	0.900	<0.001
IW-TPH-FTP	0.754	<0.001	0.832	<0.001	0.898	<0.001
IW-FTP-PP	0.621	<0.001	0.717	<0.001	0.834	<0.001
IW-FGP-PP	0.574	<0.001	0.666	<0.001	0.820	<0.001
CONUS-FGP-PP	0.419	<0.001	0.561	<0.001	0.759	<0.001
CONUS-FTP-PP	0.415	<0.001	0.559	<0.001	0.751	<0.001
IW-BMS	0.642	<0.001	0.596	<0.001	0.406	<0.001
IW-TPH	0.492	<0.001	0.500	<0.001	0.389	<0.001
IW-SDI	0.568	<0.001	0.551	<0.001	0.389	<0.001
CONUS-BMS	0.650	<0.001	0.573	<0.001	0.302	<0.001

Table 5. Regression results for the Chelan study area comparing mean cumulative MPB-caused tree mortality (TPH) from ADS and estimates of pine biomass from the CONUS (BMS-FTP and BMS-FGP) dataset and measures of pine tree density from the GNNFire vegetation datasets. Measures of pine tree density as stand density index (PSDI) and by DBH class (TPHP ≥2.54 cm, TPHP 3-25 cm, TPHP 25-50 cm, TPHP 50-75 cm, TPHP 75-100 cm, and TPH ≥100 cm) were derived from the four GNNFire map products. Vegetation variables were estimated for each LANDFIRE EVT value. Measures of stem density are shaded. Degrees of freedom in all regressions = 41.

Pine density variable	Unweighted R^2	p	Area weighted R^2	p	Mortality weighted R^2	p
GNN-SZ-PTPH-3-25	0.881	<0.001	0.949	<0.001	0.977	<0.001
GNN-SP-PTPH-3-25	0.891	<0.001	0.947	<0.001	0.976	<0.001
GNN-SP-PTPH-GE3	0.889	<0.001	0.945	<0.001	0.975	<0.001
GNN-SZ-PTPH-GE3	0.876	<0.001	0.941	<0.001	0.972	<0.001
GNN-SZ-PSDI	0.859	<0.001	0.912	<0.001	0.959	<0.001
GNN-SZ-PTPH-25-50	0.779	<0.001	0.844	<0.001	0.911	<0.001
GNN-SU-PTPH-25-50	0.712	<0.001	0.825	<0.001	0.833	<0.001
GNN-SF-PTPH-25-50	0.733	<0.001	0.830	<0.001	0.822	<0.001
GNN-SF-PSDI	0.763	<0.001	0.833	<0.001	0.812	<0.001
GNN-SU-PSDI	0.776	<0.001	0.826	<0.001	0.793	<0.001
CONUS-BMS-FTP	0.475	<0.001	0.459	<0.001	0.773	<0.001
GNN-SF-PTPH-GE3	0.725	<0.001	0.797	<0.001	0.765	<0.001
GNN-SF-PTPH-3-25	0.718	<0.001	0.788	<0.001	0.755	<0.001
GNN-SU-PTPH-GE3	0.740	<0.001	0.769	<0.001	0.712	<0.001
GNN-SU-PTPH-3-25	0.735	<0.001	0.756	<0.001	0.700	<0.001
GNN-SP-PTPH-25-50	0.512	<0.001	0.696	<0.001	0.674	<0.001
CONUS-BMS-FGP	0.331	<0.001	0.189	0.004	0.490	<0.001
GNN-SZ-PTPH-GE100	0.207	0.002	0.458	<0.001	0.253	0.001
GNN-SU-PTPH-75-100	0.036	0.221	0.221	0.001	0.054	0.158
GNN-SZ-PTPH-75-100	0.013	0.469	0.181	0.004	0.051	0.172
GNN-SP-PTPH-75-100	0.040	0.199	0.188	0.004	0.036	0.255
GNN-SF-PTPH-75-100	0.031	0.259	0.189	0.004	0.022	0.378
GNN-SP-PTPH-50-75	0.206	0.002	0.409	<0.001	0.016	0.453
GNN-SZ-PTPH-50-75	0.047	0.161	0.251	0.001	0.010	0.560
GNN-SF-PTPH-GE100	0.143	0.012	0.331	<0.001	0.007	0.609
GNN-SF-PTPH-50-75	0.126	0.019	0.345	<0.001	0.004	0.708
GNN-SP-PTPH-GE100	0.171	0.006	0.333	<0.001	0.003	0.736
GNN-SP-PSDI	0.238	0.001	0.398	<0.001	0.003	0.737
GNN-SU-PTPH-50-75	0.118	0.024	0.336	<0.001	0.000	0.907
GNN-SU-PTPH-GE100	0.123	0.021	0.343	<0.001	0.000	0.930

Table 6. Regression results for the Chelan study area comparing mean cumulative MPB-caused tree mortality (TPH) from ADS and estimates of proportion pine from the CONUS (FTP-PP and FGP-PP) and GNNFire vegetation (GNN-SZ-PP, GNN-SP-PP, GNN-SF-PP, and GNN-SU-PP) datasets. Vegetation variables were estimated for each LANDFIRE EVT value. Degrees of freedom in all regressions = 41.

Proportion pine variable	Unweighted R^2	p	Area weighted R^2	p	Mortality weighted R^2	p
GNN-SU-PP	0.527	<0.001	0.700	<0.001	0.706	<0.001
GNN-SF-PP	0.501	<0.001	0.694	<0.001	0.701	<0.001
GNN-SZ-PP	0.386	<0.001	0.519	<0.001	0.543	<0.001
GNN-SP-PP	0.393	<0.001	0.522	<0.001	0.499	<0.001
CONUS-FTP-PP	0.000	0.981	0.025	0.306	0.202	0.005
CONUS-FGP-PP	0.001	0.837	0.090	0.051	0.043	0.213

Table 7. Regression results for the Chelan study area comparing mean cumulative MPB-caused tree mortality (TPH) from ADS and estimates of biomass from the CONUS (CONUS-BMS) dataset and trees per hectare from the GNN vegetation datasets. Measures of tree density as stand density index (SDI) and by DBH class (TPH ≥2.54 cm, TPH 3-25 cm, TPH 25-50 cm, TPH 50-75 cm, TPH 75-100 cm, and TPH ≥100 cm) were derived from the four GNN map products. Vegetation variables were estimated for each LANDFIRE EVT value. Measures of stem density are shaded. Degrees of freedom in all regressions = 41.

Overall density variable	Unweighted R^2	p	Area weighted R^2	p	Mortality weighted R^2	p
GNN-SP-TPH-3-25	0.625	<0.001	0.759	<0.001	0.727	<0.001
GNN-SP-TPH-GE3	0.603	<0.001	0.749	<0.001	0.704	<0.001
GNN-SZ-TPH-3-25	0.559	<0.001	0.718	<0.001	0.600	<0.001
GNN-SZ-TPH-GE3	0.545	<0.001	0.711	<0.001	0.582	<0.001
GNN-SP-SDI	0.494	<0.001	0.693	<0.001	0.578	<0.001
GNN-SU-TPH-3-25	0.576	<0.001	0.704	<0.001	0.548	<0.001
GNN-SU-TPH-GE3	0.564	<0.001	0.705	<0.001	0.543	<0.001
GNN-SZ-SDI	0.488	<0.001	0.688	<0.001	0.538	<0.001
GNN-SF-TPH-3-25	0.517	<0.001	0.697	<0.001	0.520	<0.001
GNN-SF-TPH-GE3	0.512	<0.001	0.697	<0.001	0.511	<0.001
GNN-SU-SDI	0.501	<0.001	0.694	<0.001	0.507	<0.001
GNN-SU-TPH-25-50	0.469	<0.001	0.681	<0.001	0.479	<0.001
GNN-SF-SDI	0.473	<0.001	0.686	<0.001	0.466	<0.001
GNN-SZ-TPH-25-50	0.449	<0.001	0.652	<0.001	0.458	<0.001
GNN-SF-TPH-25-50	0.458	<0.001	0.676	<0.001	0.430	<0.001
CONUS-BMS	0.370	<0.001	0.579	<0.001	0.337	<0.001
GNN-SF-TPH-50-75	0.236	0.001	0.517	<0.001	0.094	0.062
GNN-SU-TPH-50-75	0.240	0.001	0.519	<0.001	0.088	0.071
GNN-SP-TPH-50-75	0.230	0.001	0.490	<0.001	0.087	0.072
GNN-SZ-TPH-50-75	0.171	0.006	0.457	<0.001	0.025	0.346
GNN-SF-TPH-75-100	0.098	0.041	0.347	<0.001	0.014	0.473
GNN-SP-TPH-GE100	0.094	0.045	0.243	0.001	0.010	0.547
GNN-SZ-TPH-75-100	0.075	0.076	0.268	<0.001	0.008	0.589
GNN-SU-TPH-GE100	0.076	0.073	0.331	<0.001	0.005	0.676
GNN-SF-TPH-GE100	0.039	0.203	0.197	0.003	0.003	0.765
GNN-SZ-TPH-GE100	0.044	0.177	0.279	<0.001	0.002	0.790
GNN-SU-TPH-75-100	0.134	0.016	0.425	<0.001	0.002	0.814
GNN-SP-TPH-25-50	0.179	0.005	0.419	<0.001	0.001	0.847
GNN-SP-TPH-75-100	0.127	0.019	0.382	<0.001	0.000	0.921

Sawtooth and Colorado Study Areas

In the Sawtooth study area, the average cumulative density of pines killed by MPB per EVT was best explained by pine density variables from the IW dataset, including two measures of pine biomass (IW-BMS-FGP and IW-BMS-FTP) and two measures of pine stem density (IW-SDI-FGP and IW-TPH-FGP) (mortality-weighted $R^2 > 0.90$). Variables describing proportion pine were slightly less correlated with MPB impact, although proportion pine estimates based on IW data (IW-FTP-PP and IW-FGP-PP) explained more than 87% of the variation in mean cumulative MPB impact in the Sawtooth study area (table 3). Similar results were seen for the Colorado study area where estimates of pine biomass (CONUS-BMS-FTP, CONUS-BMS-FGP, IW-BMS-FGP, and IW-BMS-FTP) and stem density (IW-SDI-FGP, IW-TPH-FTP, and IW-TPH-FTP) were highly correlated with MPB impact (mortality-weighted $R^2 > 0.90$) (table 4). Estimates of proportion pine explained more than 75% of the variation in MPB impact at the Colorado study area. At both study areas, measures of total tree density were found to be much less significant in explaining MPB impact with R^2 values less than 0.40 (tables 3 and 4). MPB impact at both study areas was most correlated with estimates of pine biomass (tables 3 and 4). Our overall goal, however, was to derive estimates of pine density rather than biomass. Of the pine density measures evaluated, pine TPH estimates derived from IW-FGP and IW-FTP vegetation models were found to be the most closely correlated with MPB impact and, therefore, MPB host availability in both study areas.

Mean pine TPH derived from IW-FGP, the most highly correlated variable, showed a high association with mean cumulative MPB impact across all LANDFIRE EVT values used for the units of analysis in the regression equations for the Sawtooth study area (fig. 7), and for the EVTs comprising the majority of the Colorado study area (fig. 8). Estimates of pine stem density for four EVTs in the Colorado study area (Southern Rocky Mountain Mesic Montane Mixed Conifer Forest and Woodland, Southern Rocky Mountain Dry-Mesic Montane Mixed Conifer Forest and Woodland, Southern Rocky Mountain Ponderosa Pine Woodland, and Rocky Mountain Montane Riparian Systems) poorly described MPB-caused tree mortality. These same EVTs also had poor association between proportion pine estimates and MPB-caused tree mortality in the Colorado study area (fig. 9). Proportion pine estimates for the Sawtooth study area were closely associated with MPB impact except for the Barren and Northern Rocky Mountain Subalpine Deciduous Shrubland EVTs (fig. 10). Greatest mean MPB impact was associated with the Rocky Mountain Lodgepole Pine Forest EVT in the Colorado study area and Rocky Mountain Poor-Site Lodgepole Pine Forest EVT in the Sawtooth study area (figs. 7 and 8).

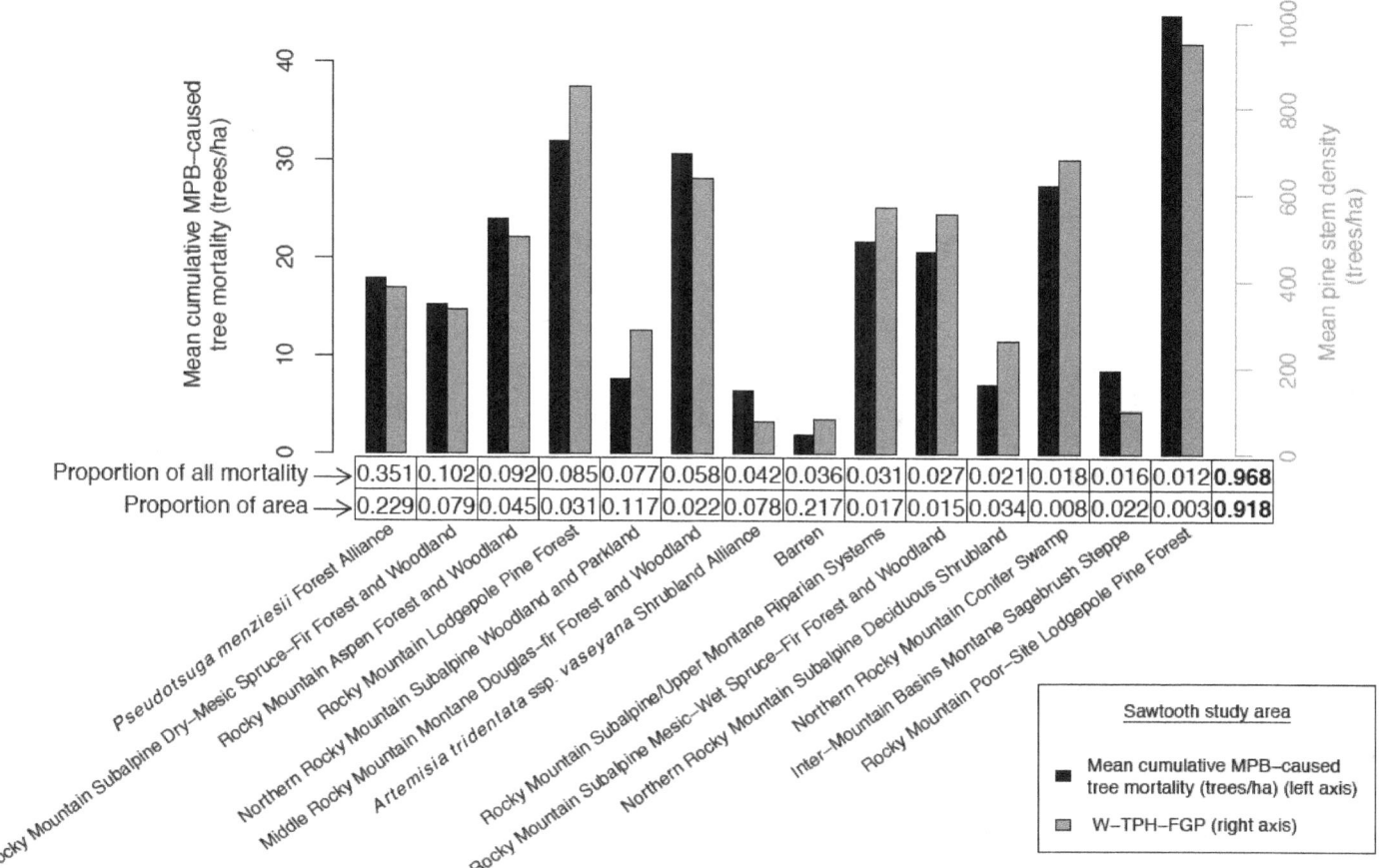

Figure 7. Comparison of pine density estimates and mean cumulative MPB-caused tree mortality (TPH) across the 14 EVTs with the largest amount of MPB impact, Sawtooth study area. Pine density estimates are based on the IW-TPH-FGP vegetation model (see table 1). These EVTs experienced 96.8% of all MPB impact and constitute 92% of all area in the Sawtooth study area.

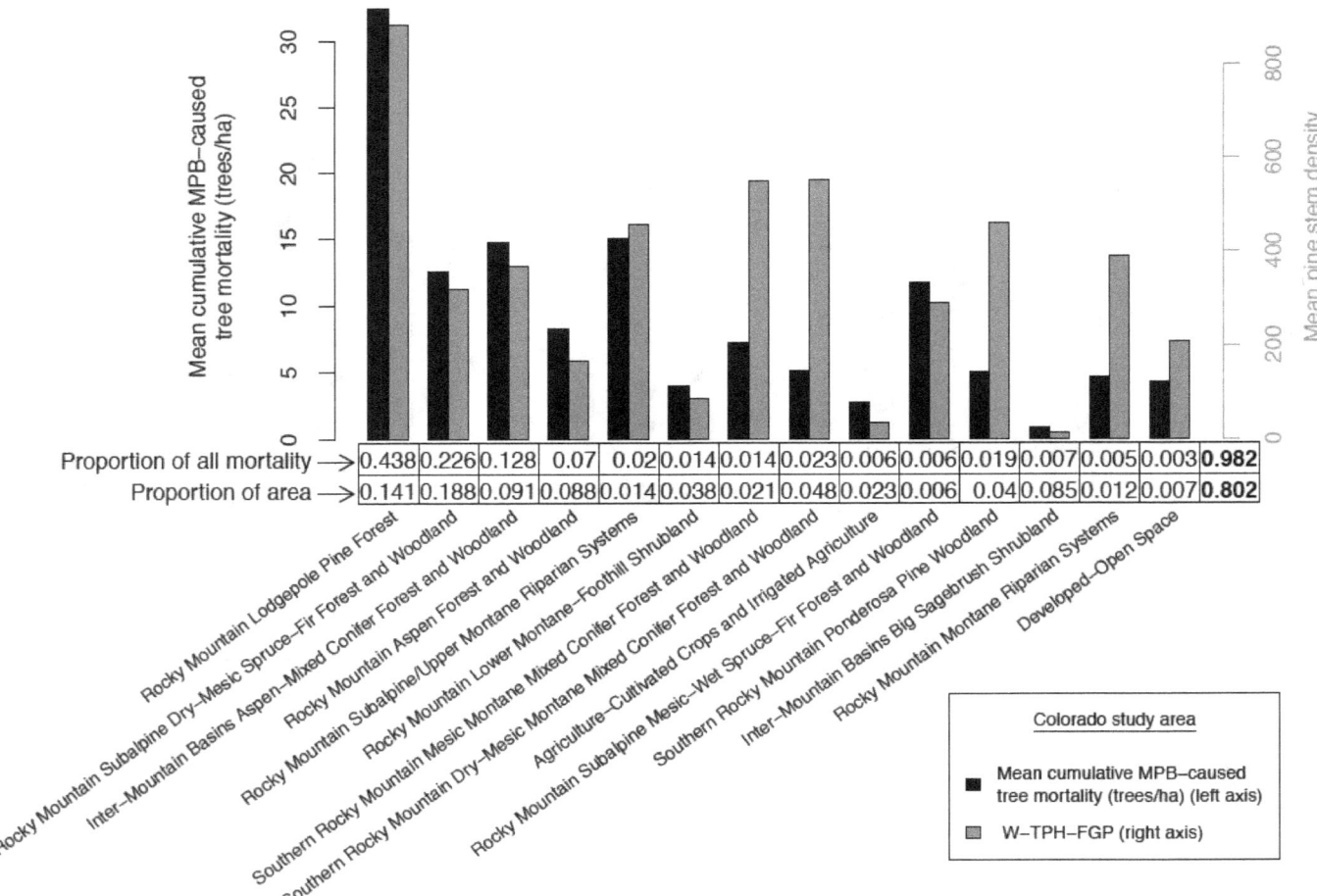

Figure 8. Comparison of pine density estimate and mean cumulative MPB-caused tree mortality (TPH) across the 14 EVTs with the largest amount of MPB impact, Colorado study area. Pine density estimates are based on the IW-TPH-FGP vegetation model (see table 1). These EVTs experienced 98.2% of all MPB impact and constitute 80.2% of all area in the Colorado study area.

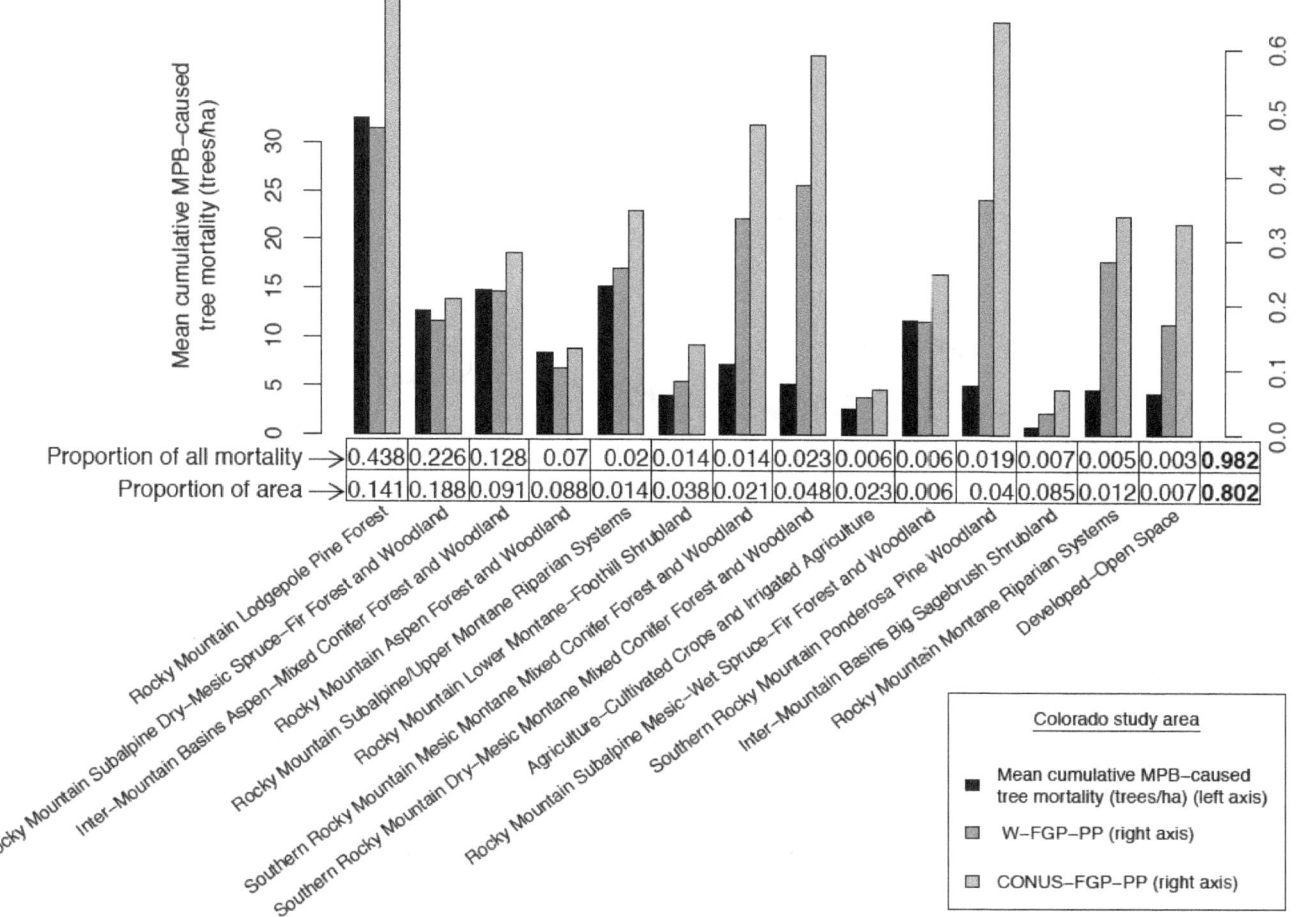

Figure 9. Comparison of proportion pine estimates and mean cumulative MPB-caused tree mortality (TPH) across the 14 EVTs with the largest amount of MPB impact, Colorado study area. Proportion pine estimates are based on the IW-FGP-PP and CONUS-FGP-PP vegetation models (see table 1). These EVTs experienced 98.2% of all MPB impact and constitute 80.2% of all area in the Colorado study area.

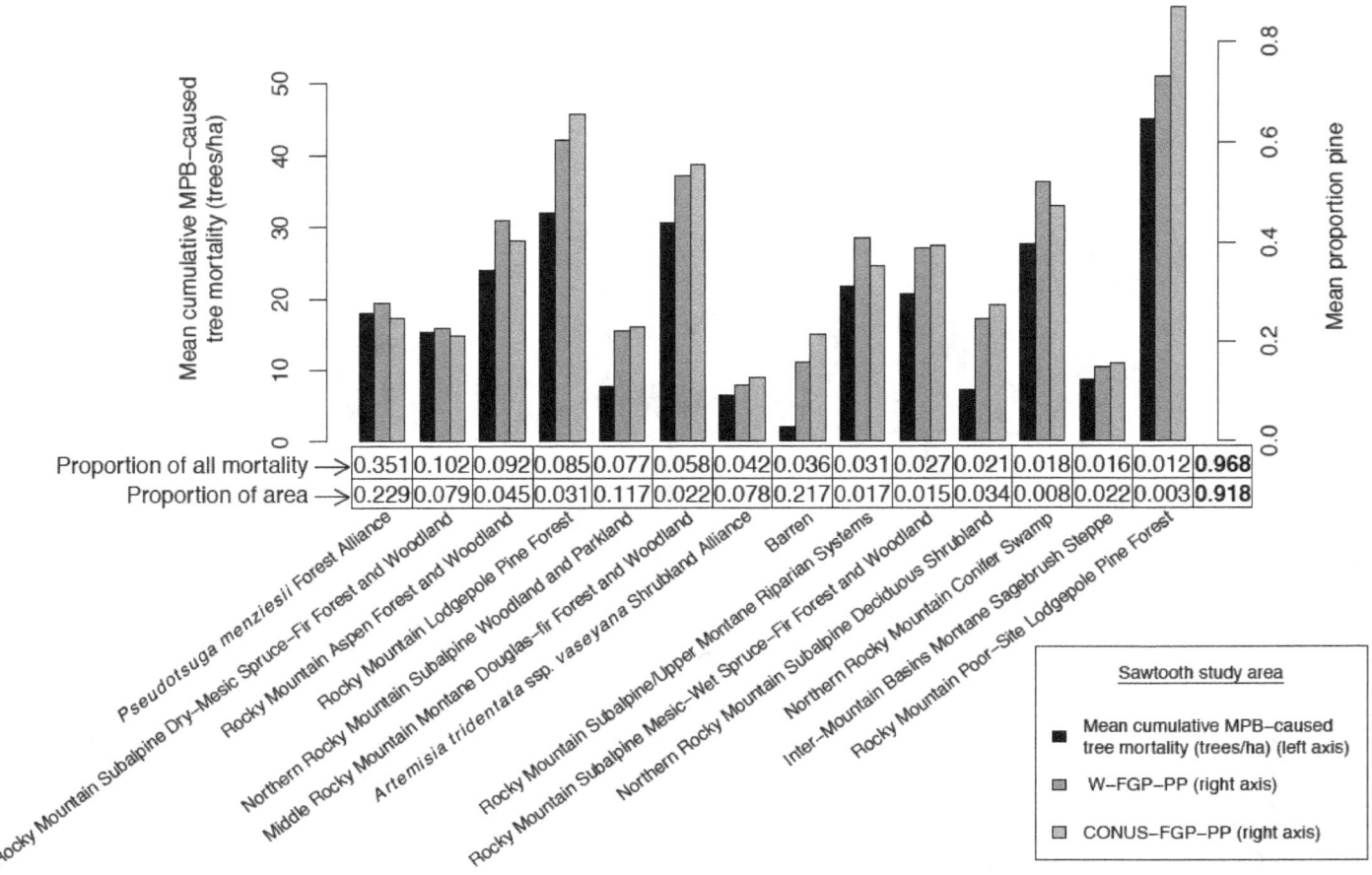

Figure 10. Comparison of proportion pine estimates and mean cumulative MPB-caused tree mortality (TPH) across the 14 EVTs with the largest amount of MPB impact, Sawtooth study area. Proportion pine estimates are based on the IW-FGP-PP and CONUS-FGP-PP vegetation models (see table 1). These EVTs experienced 96.8% of all MPB impact and constitute 92% of all area in the Sawtooth study area.

Chelan Study Area

The Chelan study area was covered by the CONUS and GNN vegetation datasets, and a total of 65 vegetation estimates were developed (tables 5, 6, and 7). Of all vegetation models evaluated, estimates of pine density in units of TPH derived from the GNN species (GNN-SP) and species size (GNN-SZ) models (GNN-SP-PTPH-3-25, GNN-SP-PTPH-GE3, GNN-SZ-PTPH-3-25, and GNN-SZ-PTPH-GE3) were most highly correlated with MPB impact based on a mortality-weighted R^2 (table 5). These models explained ~97% of the variation in mean cumulative MPB impact per EVT. Pine SDI (GNN-SZ-PSDI) and a measure of pine TPH in the larger DBH size classes (GNN-SZ-PTPH-25-50) were also highly significant, explaining more than 90% of the variation (table 5). Measures of proportion pine based on the GNN structure models (GNN-SU-PP and GNN-SF-PP) and measures of total tree density based on the GNN SP model (GNN-SP-TPH-3-25, and GNN-SP-TPH-GE3) were also reasonably well correlated with MPB impact, explaining at least 70% of the variation in mean cumulative MPB impact per EVT (tables 6 and 7). When all vegetation estimates (pine density, total tree density, and proportion pine) are considered, predictions from the GNN vegetation datasets were more correlated with MPB impact than predictions from the CONUS vegetation dataset. Mean pine TPH derived from the GNN species size dataset (GNN-SZ-PTPH-GE3, $R^2 = 0.972$) showed a high association with mean cumulative MPB impact across all LANDFIRE EVT values used for the units of analysis in the regression equations for the Chelan study area (fig. 11). Proportion pine estimates by EVT class are less well associated with all EVTs (fig. 12). Greatest mean cumulative MPB impact was associated with the Rocky Mountain Lodgepole Pine Forest EVT (fig. 11).

Relationship Between EVT Area and Amount of MPB Impact

In linear regressions used to determine the strength of the relationship between cumulative MPB impact and estimates of pine and total tree density and pine and total biomass from the three vegetation datasets (see above), the landscape unit of analyses was the Landfire EVT classification. To test if the area represented by a particular EVT (i.e., size) in each study area was a significant contributor to the correlation between EVTs and MPB impact, we regressed the area (hectares) of each EVT on cumulative MPB-caused tree mortality. In the Sawtooth study area, the area encompassed by particular EVTs only explained ~54% of the variability in cumulative MPB-caused tree mortality, and one of the largest EVTs had very little tree mortality (fig. 13). In the Colorado study area, the area of each EVT explained about 66% of the variation, and the two EVTs encompassing the largest area also experienced the highest cumulative MPB-caused tree mortality (fig. 14). In the Chelan study area, the presence of one very large EVT (Northern Rocky Mountain Dry-Mesic Montane Mixed Conifer Forest), which encompassed 35.1% of the landscape, contributed to a very high R^2 value (0.888) from the regression of EVT size on cumulative MPB-caused tree mortality (fig. 15). After excluding this EVT, the R^2 value fell to 0.35, and no clear trend existed between EVT size and total MPB impact per EVT (fig. 16). These low R^2 values indicate that EVT size is not highly correlated with cumulative MPB impact, suggesting that EVT classifications identify vegetation types consequential to MPB dynamics.

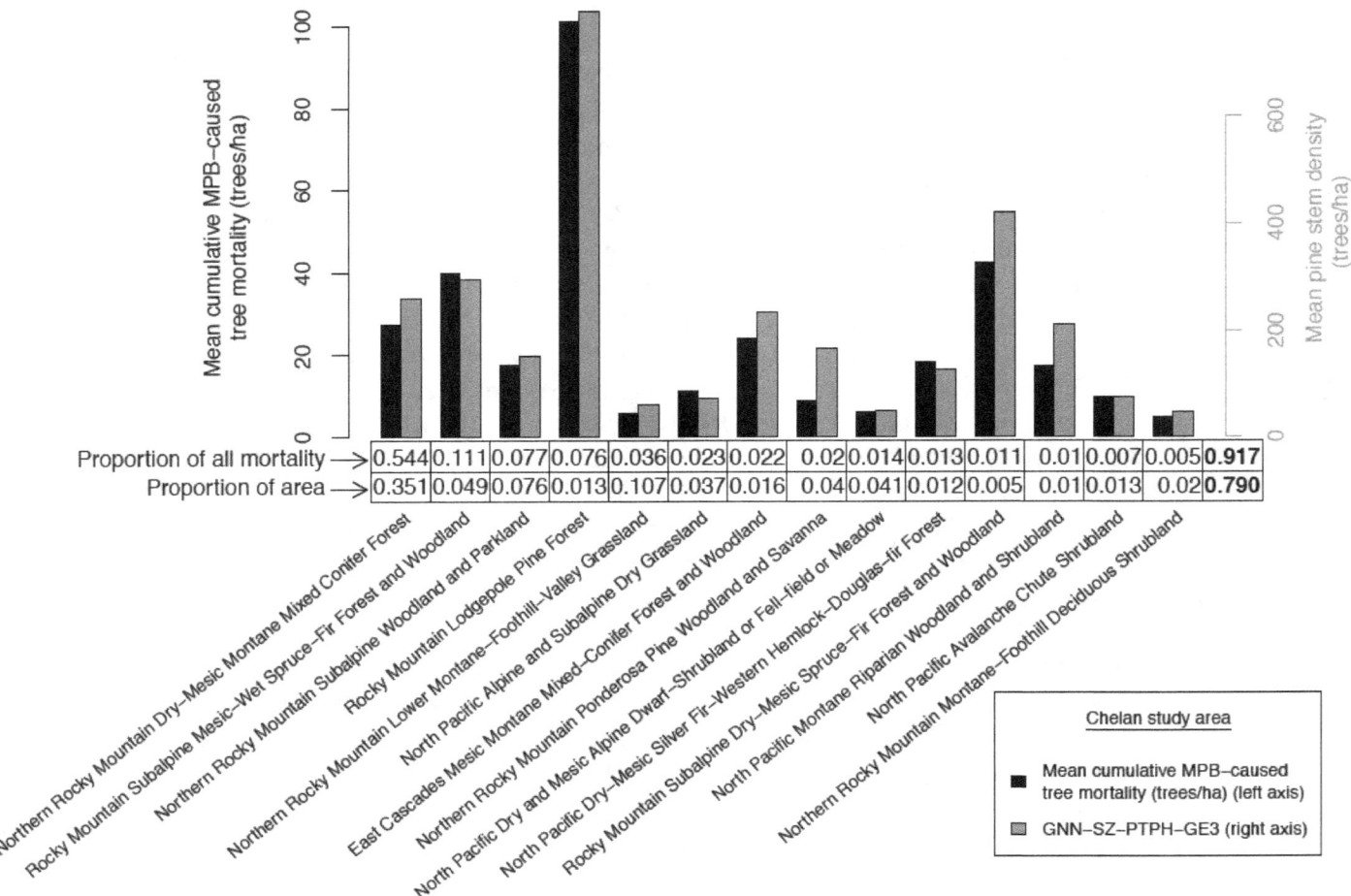

Figure 11. Comparison of pine density estimate and mean cumulative MPB-caused tree mortality (TPH) across the 14 EVTs with the largest amount of MPB impact, Chelan study area. Pine density estimate is from the GNN-SZ-PTHP-GE3 vegetation model (see table 1). These EVTs experienced 91.7% of all MPB impact and constitute 79% of all area in the Chelan study area.

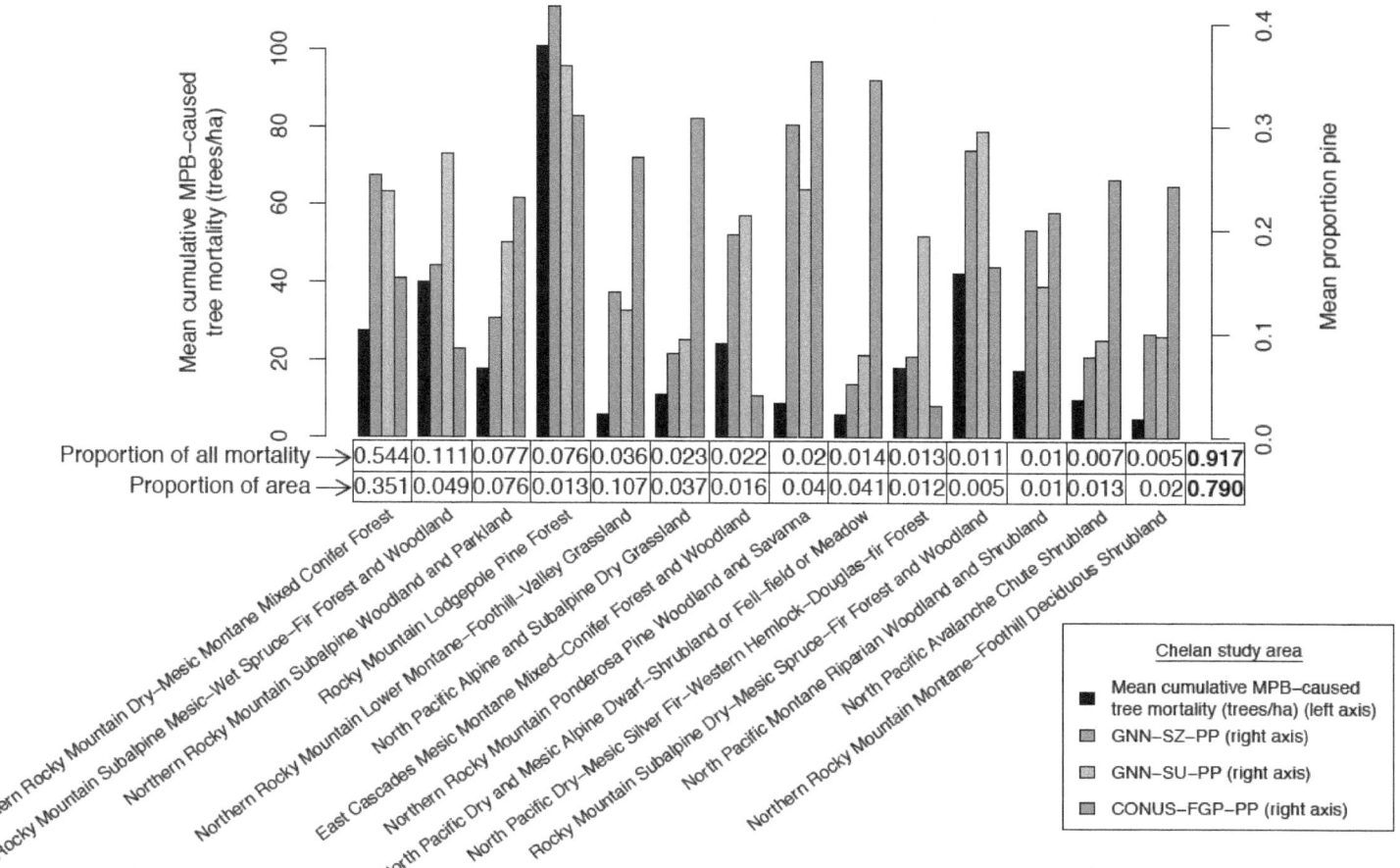

Figure 12. Comparison of proportion pine estimates and mean cumulative MPB-caused tree mortality (TPH) across the 14 EVTs with the largest amount of MPB impact, Chelan study area. Proportion pine estimates are from the GNN-SZ-PP, GNN-SU-PP, and CONUS-FGP-PP vegetation models (see table 1). These EVTs experienced 91.7% of all MPB impact and constitute 79% of all area in the Chelan study area.

Sawtooth study area:
EVT area vs. MPB–caused tree mortality

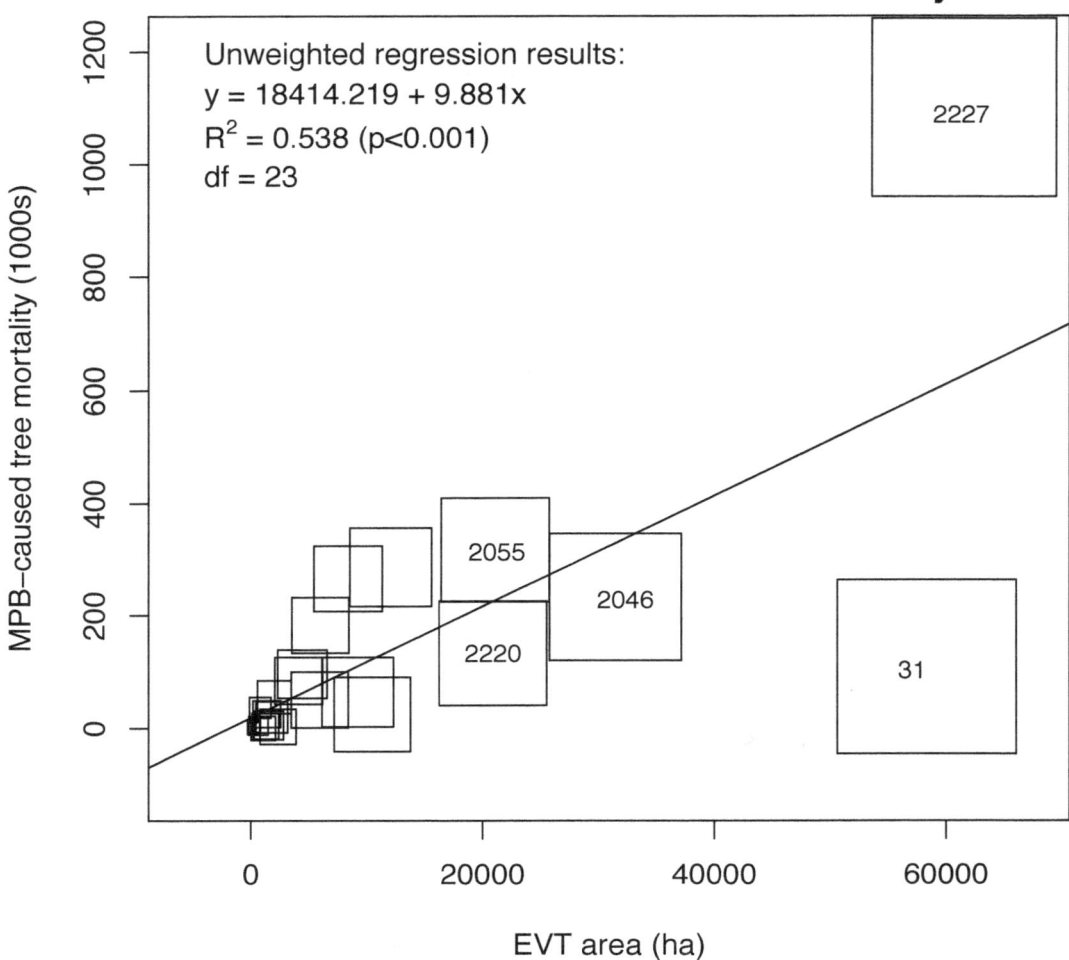

Unweighted regression results:

$y = 18414.219 + 9.881x$

$R^2 = 0.538$ (p<0.001)

df = 23

Figure 13. Total MPB-caused tree mortality (from ADS) in the Sawtooth study area as a function of the area of each LANDFIRE EVT (see table 2) in the study area. Square size is proportional to area of each EVT. The weak correlation between EVT area and total tree mortality suggests that EVT classifications, rather than area size alone, capture ecological conditions consequential to MPB dynamics. Labeled EVT classes are: 31: Barren; 2046: Northern Rocky Mountain Subalpine Woodland and Parkland; 2055: Rocky Mountain Subalpine Dry-Mesic Spruce-Fir Forest and Woodland; 2220: *Artemisia tridentata* ssp. *vaseyana* Shrubland Alliance; and 2227: *Pseudotsuga menziesii* Forest Alliance.

Colorado study area:
EVT area vs. MPB–caused tree mortality

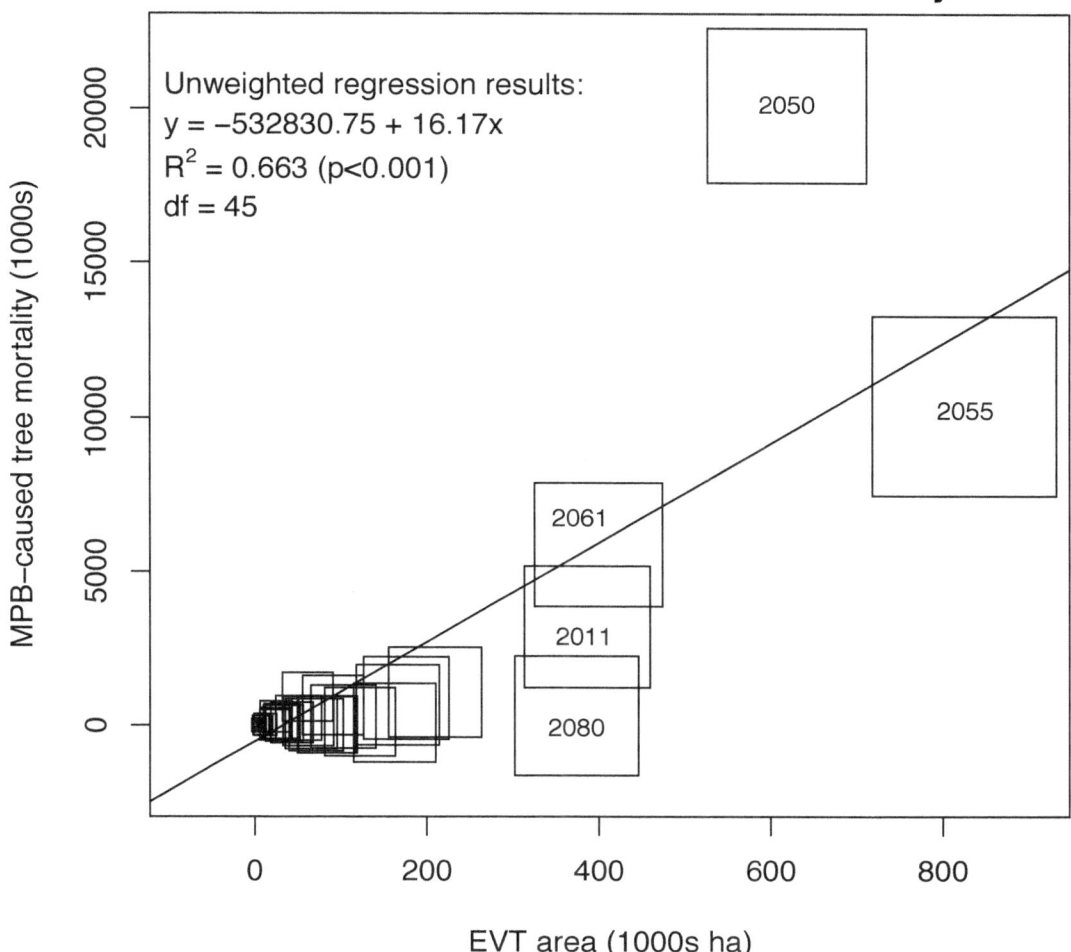

Unweighted regression results:
y = −532830.75 + 16.17x
R^2 = 0.663 (p<0.001)
df = 45

Figure 14. Total MPB-caused tree mortality (from ADS) in the Colorado study area as a function of the area of each EVT (see table 2) in the study area (from LANDFIRE). Square size is proportional to area of each EVT. The weak correlation between EVT area and total tree mortality suggests that EVT classifications, rather than area size alone, capture ecological conditions consequential to MPB dynamics. Labeled EVT classes are: 2011: Rocky Mountain Aspen Forest and Woodland; 2050: Rocky Mountain Lodgepole Pine Forest; 2055: Rocky Mountain Subalpine Dry-Mesic Spruce-Fir Forest and Woodland; 2061: Inter-Mountain Basins Aspen-Mixed Conifer Forest and Woodland; and 2080: Inter-Mountain Basins Big Sagebrush Shrubland.

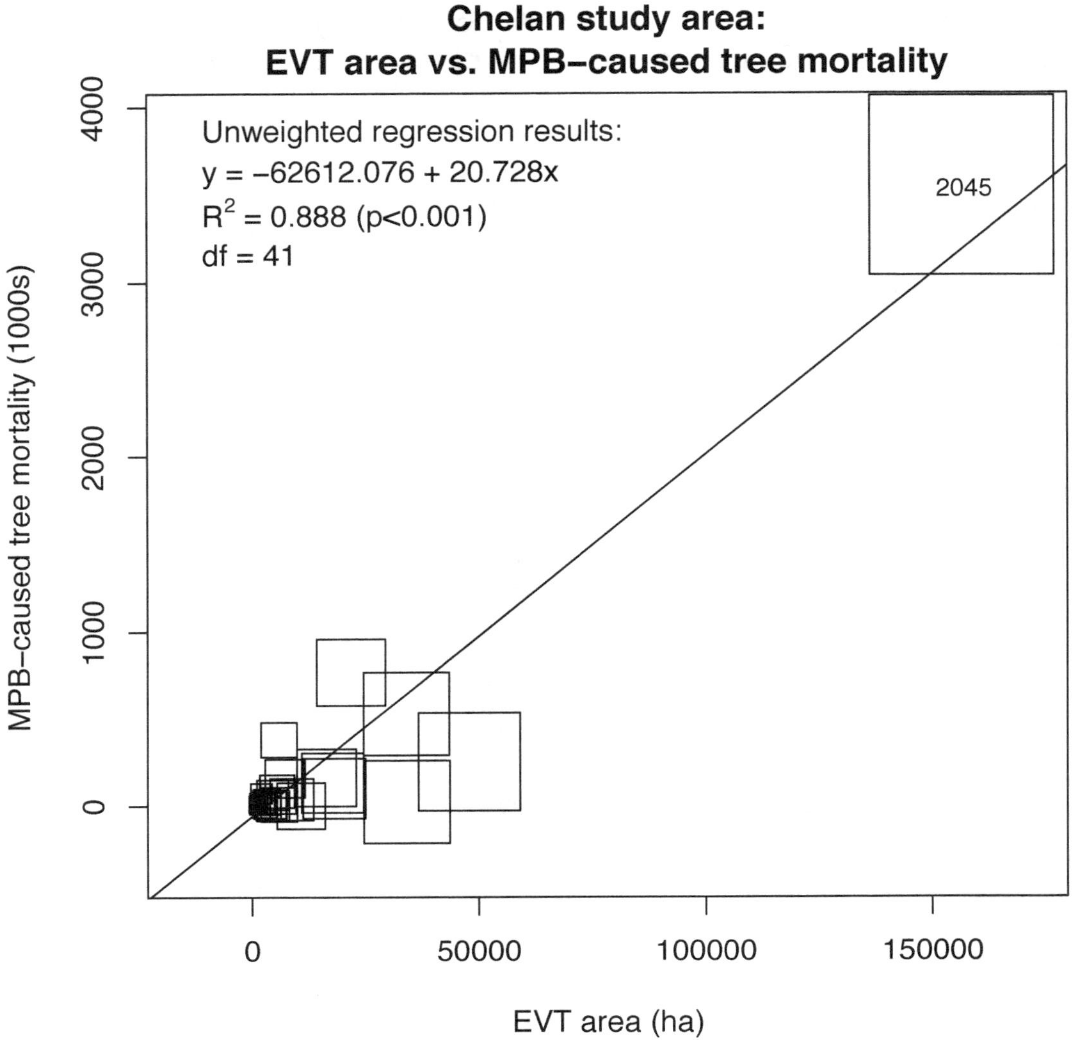

Figure 15. Total MPB-caused tree mortality (from ADS) in the Chelan study area as a function of the area of each EVT (see table 2) in the study area (from LANDFIRE). Square size is proportional to area of each EVT. The large EVT labeled "2045" (Northern Rocky Mountain Dry-Mesic Montane Mixed Conifer Forest) encompasses 35.1% of the study area and contributed to a large R^2 value. When this large EVT is excluded from the regression of EVT area on total MPB-caused tree mortality, the R^2 value falls to 0.351, indicating that EVT area size is not a good predictor of total MPB-caused tree mortality and suggesting that EVT classifications capture ecological conditions consequential to MPB dynamics.

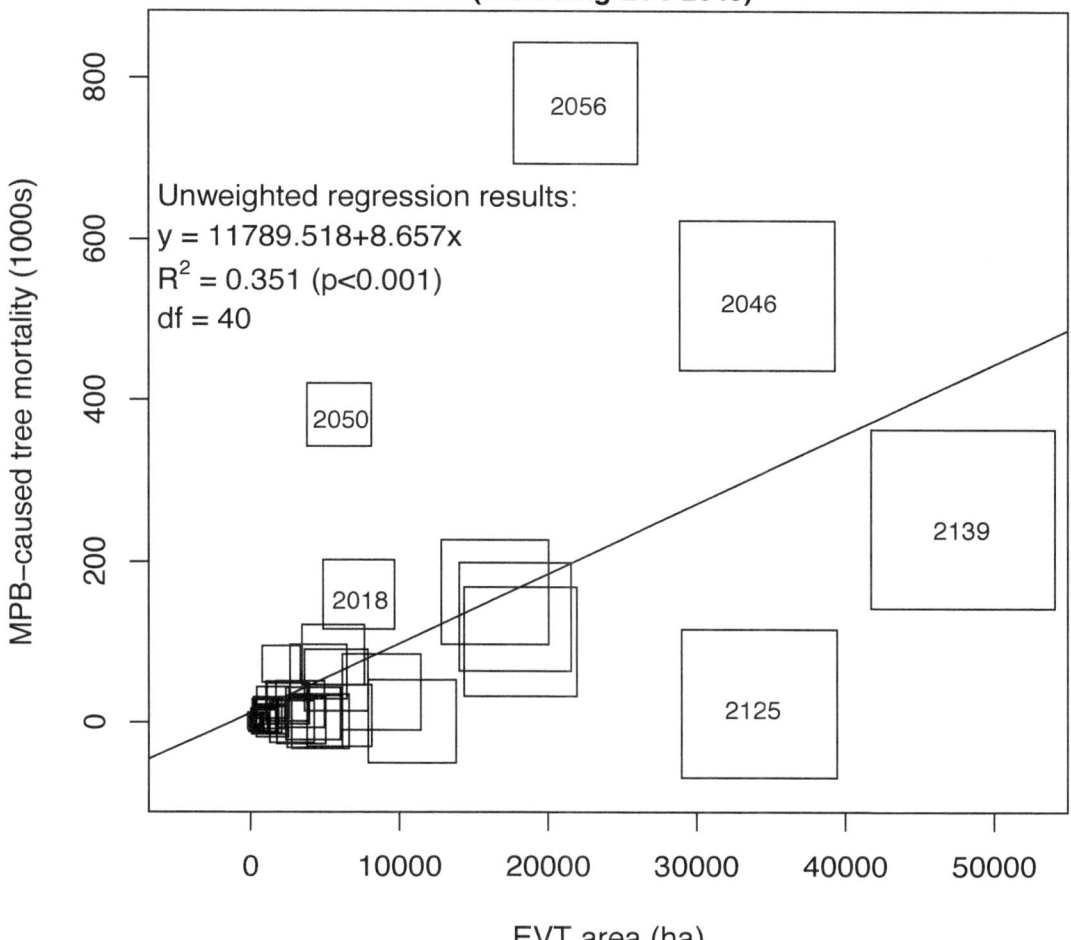

Chelan study area:
EVT area vs. MPB-caused tree mortality
(excluding EVT 2045)

Unweighted regression results:
$y = 11789.518 + 8.657x$
$R^2 = 0.351$ (p<0.001)
df = 40

2056
2046
2050
2139
2018
2125

MPB-caused tree mortality (1000s)

EVT area (ha)

Figure 16. Total MPB-caused tree mortality (from ADS) in the Chelan study area as a function of the area of each EVT (see table 2) in the study area (from LANDFIRE). Square size is proportional to area of each EVT. This regression and scatterplot exclude the large EVT Northern Rocky Mountain Dry-Mesic Montane Mixed Conifer Forest, which encompasses 35.1% of the study area. The weak correlation between EVT area and total tree mortality suggest that EVT classifications, rather than area size alone, capture ecological conditions consequential to MPB dynamics. Labeled EVT classes are: 2018: East Cascades Mesic Montane Mixed-Conifer Forest and Woodland; 2046: Northern Rocky Mountain Subalpine Woodland and Parkland; 2050: Rocky Mountain Lodgepole Pine Forest; 2056: Rocky Mountain Subalpine Mesic-Wet Spruce-Fir Forest and Woodland; 2125: Inter-Mountain Basins Big Sagebrush Steppe; and 2139: Northern Rocky Mountain Lower Montane-Foothill-Valley Grassland.

Total tree and pine only density estimates are highly explanatory of MPB impact when measured across LANDFIRE EVTs. Moreover, the pine density estimates were generally more highly correlated with MPB impact than estimates of overall tree density. However, high levels of correlation between pine density and observed MPB impact when measured across EVTs does not necessarily indicate that EVTs delineate vegetation types of consequence to MPB impact. If high levels of correlation between the pine density models and observed MPB impact persist when measured across other zones of analysis, this would indicate that EVTs do not intrinsically parse the landscape into delineations consequential to MPB dynamics. Rather, the EVTs would accidentally capture MPB impact simply due to their prevalence on the landscape. In this case, EVTs would be poor units of analysis with which to assess our vegetation models. We tested this by producing 1000 random landscapes for each study area such that each landscape was composed of classes of analogous to LANDFIRE EVTs in number, size distribution, and spatial contiguity. For each study area, the 1000 sets of random classes were used as units of analysis to assess the explanatory power of pine density estimates with respect to mean cumulative MPB impact per class using unweighted, area-weighted, and mortality-weighted regressions. The pine density estimates used were IW-TPH-FGP for the Sawtooth and Colorado study areas and GNN-SZ-PTPH-GE3 in the Chelan study area.

In the Sawtooth study area, the use of units of analysis defined by LANDFIRE EVTs resulted in higher un-weighted, area-weighed, and mortality-weighted R^2 values than did random classes in more than 99.4% of the random landscapes tested (n = 1000) (fig. 17). We found similar results for the Colorado study area where the unweighted, area-weighed, and mortality-weighted R^2 values using EVTs resulted in higher values in 89%, 98%, and 99% of the random landscapes, respectively (fig. 17). In the Chelan study area, the use of units of analysis defined by LAND-FIRE EVTs resulted in higher R^2 values than did random classes in 100% of the random landscapes tested (fig. 17). These results suggest that EVTs are reasonable units of analysis for assessing the correlation between pine TPH estimates derived from the IW and GNN vegetation datasets and observed patterns of MPB-caused tree mortality from ADS.

Discussion and Conclusions

Our overall goal was to develop spatially explicit datasets of pine tree density for use in predicting MPB distribution and population spread. Using geospatial datasets of vegetation composition and structure that are available for the conterminous United States (IW and CONUS; table 1) and portions of the western United States (GNN; table 1), in addition to LANDFIRE EVTs, we developed a simple method for estimating pine and total tree density and biomass at a 30-m spatial resolution. Essentially, the ecological information encoded in the LANDFIRE EVTs provided information that can be used to downscale pine density data. Three study areas in

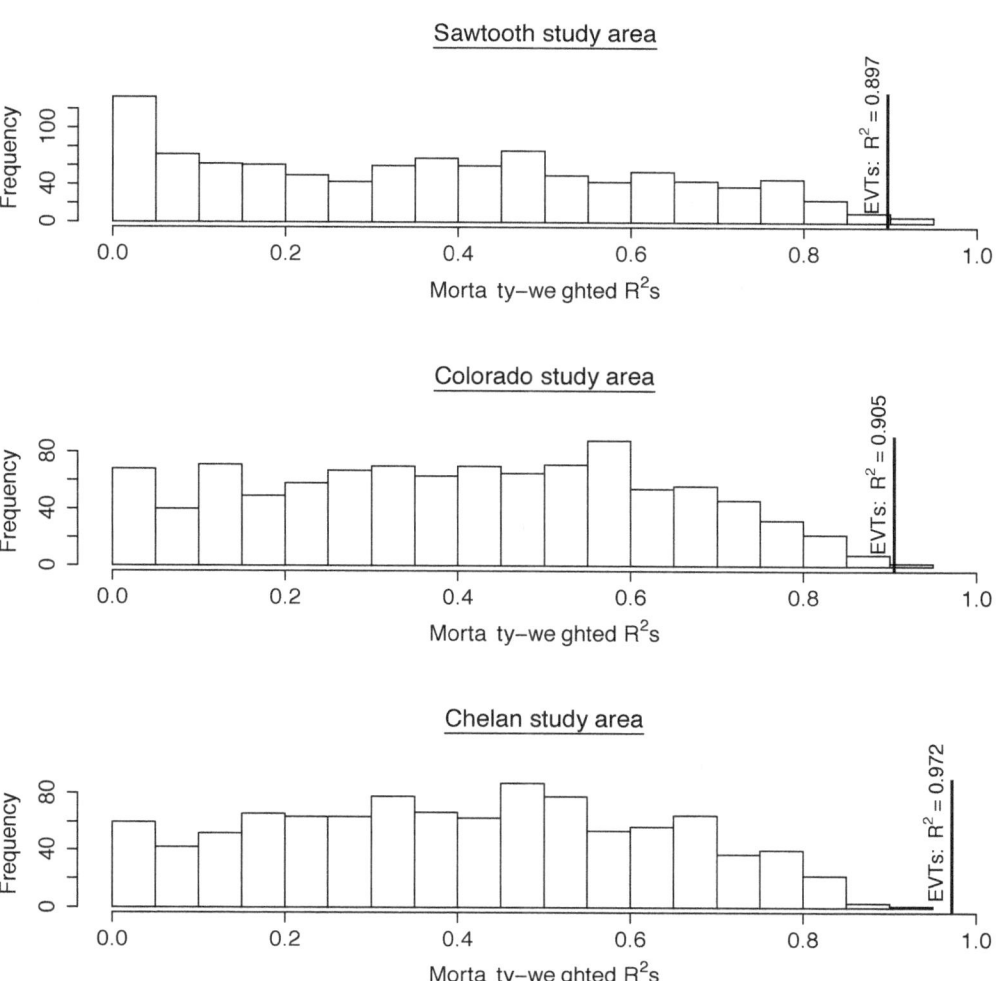

Figure 17. Assessment of EVTs as units of analysis through comparison with random landscapes (n = 1000). Regressions compared pine density estimate IW-TPH-FGP and mean cumulative MPB-caused tree mortality using randomly generated classes as units of analysis. Vertical lines on the histograms indicate the R^2 value derived from the use of EVTs as units of analysis. For the Sawtooth, Colorado, and Chelan study areas, the EVT-derived mortality-weighted R^2 was greater than 994, 998, and 1000 R^2s derived from random landscapes, respectively.

the western United States that have experienced recent MPB outbreaks were used for model assessment. Because pines are the main host of MPB, we assumed that indices of MPB impact based on ADS provided a spatially relevant estimate of host tree availability. Using LANDFIRE EVTs as the units of analysis, we determined how well our estimates of pine and total tree density and biomass (30-m resolution) explained variation in observed MPB-caused tree mortality derived from ADS. Because our goal was to develop vegetation data that can be used to drive a spatial model of MPB population success, ADS data are particularly appropriate in spite of potential inherent inaccuracies.

Correlation coefficients, weighted by the area of observed MPB-caused tree mortality, show that pine TPH estimates derived from IW-FGP vegetation model were the most closely correlated with MPB impact (mortality-weighted $R^2 = 0.90$), and therefore MPB host availability, in the Sawtooth and Colorado study areas. In the Chelan study area, estimates of pine TPH derived from the GNN species and species size vegetation models were most highly correlated with MPB impact (mortality-weighted $R^2 = 0.97$). In the Colorado and Sawtooth study areas, estimates of pine biomass derived from CONUS and IW vegetation datasets were also highly correlated with MPB-caused tree mortality (mortality-weighted $R^2 > 0.93$). In some sense, the GNN approach applied in the Chelan study area more directly connects 30-m predictions with observed plot data and is probably more accurate than using LANDFIRE to downscale IW density data. However, results in Colorado and Idaho are comparable to those in Chelan, and with more than 90% of the variability in mortality impacts per EVT described by our downscaled pine density models, we are confident in their ability to predict the presence of suitable host for MPB.

Of the four EVTs in the Colorado study area in which pine density estimates were poorly correlated with MPB impacts, the three largest (and most impacted) describe vegetation types particular to the southern Rocky Mountains (Southern Rocky Mountain Mesic Montane Mixed Conifer Forest and Woodland, Southern Rocky Mountain Dry-Mesic Montane Mixed Conifer Forest and Woodland, and Southern Rocky Mountain Ponderosa Pine Woodland). These vegetation communities are concentrated along the eastern edge of the Colorado study area, a region that has only recently been impacted by MPB (fig. 18). Therefore, if MPB populations continue to spread eastward into these vegetation communities, we expect that estimates of pine density based on the vegetation datasets would become even more highly correlated with MPB-caused tree mortality.

LANDFIRE EVTs provide an index of the plant communities growing in a particular 30-m cell (USGS 2009) and were found to effectively delineate distinct vegetation types that are meaningful indicators of suitability for MPB-caused tree mortality. When compared to randomly generated landscape classifications, estimates of pine density using Landfire EVTs consistently had significantly higher correlations with MPB-caused tree mortality. Of all EVTs found in the study areas, the highest mean cumulative MPB-caused tree mortality in the Chelan and Colorado study areas was associated with the Rocky Mountain Lodgepole Pine Forest EVT and the Rocky Mountain Poor-Site Lodgepole Pine Forest EVT in the Sawtooth study area. In the Sawtooth and Chelan study areas, pine TPH estimates were highly correlated with mean cumulative MPB-caused tree mortality across all EVTs found in those study areas.

A critical transition in MPB outbreak dynamics occurs when small spots of infested trees erupt into large numbers of infested trees at watershed scales. Spatially explicit mechanistic modeling of MPB outbreaks will therefore require highly detailed spatial data on host density and distribution. GNN data, available for portions of the western United States, including our Chelan study area, provide spatially explicit estimates of pine density at 30 m and are suitable for mechanistic modeling

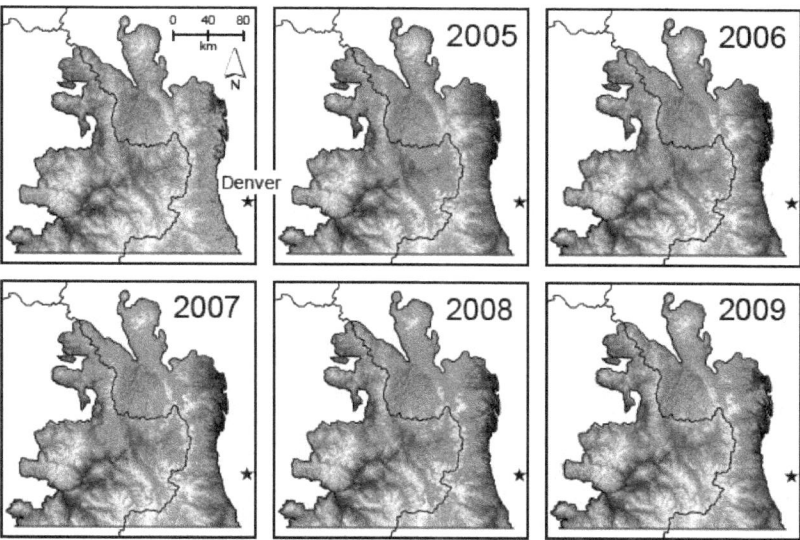

Figure 18. Area encompassed by three EVTs (Southern Rocky Mountain Mesic Montane Mixed Conifer Forest and Woodland, Southern Rocky Mountain Dry-Mesic Montane Mixed Conifer Forest and Woodland, and Southern Rocky Mountain Ponderosa Pine Woodland) where pine density estimate IW-TPH-FGP did not correlate well with mean cumulative MPB impact in the Colorado study area (green areas in top left image) (see fig. 8). Also shown is the spread of MPB impacts across the Colorado study area (based on ADS data) for years 2005-2009 (red areas). The black line indicates the continental divide. The three EVTs with poor correlation to MPB impact occur primarily on the eastern side of the study area. MPB impacts were not recorded for this area between 2005 and 2009, despite the availability of suitable hosts (see fig. 6).

of MPB outbreak dynamics. In areas where GNN data have not been developed, available geospatial datasets of vegetation are too coarse in scale (e.g., 250 m) and are not species specific. Here, we showed that it is possible to use ecologically based LANDFIRE EVTs to downscale tree density data from 250 m to 30 m to acquire estimates of pine density at spatially relevant scales for modeling tree mortality caused by MPB. This will greatly increase scientific understanding of MPB outbreak dynamics and facilitate landscape modeling of MPB population spread and resultant tree mortality.

Acknowledgments

The Western Wildland Threat Assessment Center and National Science Foundation grant DEB 0918756 provided funding for this project. ADS data were provided by USDA Forest Service FHP and its partners. Brian Howell, Jeri Lyn Harris, and Julie Johnson advised and assisted with ADS data. Dale Weyermann pointed us toward the GNN dataset. Jock Blackard assisted with the IW datasets. We thank Janet Ohlman and Jock Blackard for helpful reviews of this manuscript.

References

Bentz, B.J. 2006. Mountain pine beetle population sampling: inferences from Lindgren pheromone traps and tree emergence cages. Canadian Journal of Forest Research. 36(2):351-360.

Bentz, B.J.; Bracewell, R.B.; Mock, K.E.; Pfrender, M.E. 2011. Genetic architecture and phenotypic plasticity of thermally-regulated traits in an eruptive species, *Dendroctonus ponderosae*. Evolutionary Ecology 25:1269-1288.

Bentz, B.J.; Logan, J.A.; Amman, G.D. 1991. Temperature dependent development of the mountain pine beetle (Coleoptera: Scolytidae), and simulation of its phenology. Canadian Entomologist. 123:1083-1094.

Bentz, B.J.; Mullins, D.E. 1999. Ecology of mountain pine beetle (Coleoptera: Scolytidae) cold hardening in the Intermountain West. Environmental Entomology. 28(4): 577-587.

Bentz, B.J.; Regniere, J.; Fettig, C.J.; Hansen, E. M.; Hayes, J.L.; Hicke, J.A.; Kelsey, R.G.; Negron, J.F.; Seybold, S.J. 2010. Climate change and bark beetles of the western United States and Canada: direct and indirect effects. BioScience. 60(8):602-613.

Berryman, A.A.; Stenseth, N.C.; Wollkind, D.J. 1984. Metastability of forest ecosystems infested by bark beetles. Researches on Population Ecology. 26:13-29.

Blackard, J.A. 2009. IW-FIA predicted forest attribute maps-2005. [Online]. Fort Collins, CO: U.S. Department of Agriculture, Forest Service, Rocky Mountain Research Station. Available: http://www.fs.fed.us/rm/data_archive [2009, December 10].

Blackard, J.A. 2010. Intermountain West Spatial Data Services Coordinator, USDA Forest Service, Rocky Mountain Research Station. [Email to B. Crabb]. July 12.

Blackard, J.A.; Finco, M.V.; Helmer, E.H; Holden, G.R.; [and others]. 2008. Mapping U.S. forest biomass using nationwide forest inventory data and moderate resolution information. Remote Sensing of Environment. 112:1658-1677.

Comer, P.; Faber-Langendoen, D.; Evans, R; Gawler, S.; Josse, C.; Kittel, G.; Menard, S.; Pyne, M.; Reid, M.; Schulz, K.; Snow, K.; Teague, J. 2003. Ecological systems of the United States: a working classification of U.S. terrestrial systems. Arlington, VA: NatureServe. 75 p.

Drury, S.A.; Herynk, J.M. 2011. The national tree-list layer. Gen. Tech. Rep. RMRS-GTR-254. Fort Collins, CO: U.S. Department of Agriculture, Forest Service, Rocky Mountain Research Station. 26 p.

Environmental Systems Research Institute [ESRI]. 2008. ArcGIS desktop: release 9.3. Redlands, CA: Environmental Systems Research Institute.

Eyre, F.H., ed. 1980. Forest cover types of the United States and Canada. Bethesda, MD: Society of American Foresters. 148 p.

Guisan, A.; Thuiller, W. 2005. Predicting species distribution: offering more than simple habitat models. Ecology Letters. 8:993-1009.

Halsey, R. 1998. Aerial detection survey metadata for the Intermountain Region 4. U.S. Department of Agriculture Forest Service, Forest Health Protection.

Homer, C.; Gallant, A. 2001. Partitioning the conterminous United States into mapping zones for Landsat TM land cover mapping. White Paper. U.S. Department of the Interior, Geological Survey.

Kearny, M; Porter, W. 2009 Mechanistic niche modelling: combining physiological and spatial data to predict species' ranges. Ecology Letters. 12:334-350.

Krist, F.J.; Sapio, F.J.; Tkacz, B.M. 2007. Mapping risk from forest insects and diseases. FHTET 2007-06. Fort Collins, CO: U.S. Department of Agriculture, Forest Service, Forest Health Protection, Forest Health Technology Team. 115 p.

LEMMA. 2005. LEMMA: the GNNFire project [Homepage of the Landscape Ecology, Modeling, Mapping & Analysis research group of the USDA Forest Service Pacific Northwest Research Station and Oregon State University]. [Online]. Available: http://www.fsl.orst.edu/lemma/main.php?project=gnnfire&id=mapProducts [October 24, 2010].

Lewis, M.A.; Nelson, W.; Xu, C. 2010. A structured threshold model for mountain pine beetle outbreak. Bulletin of Mathematical Biology. 72:565-589.

Logan, J.A.; Bentz, B.J. 1999. Model analysis of mountain pine beetle seasonality. Environmental Entomology. 28:924-934.

Long, J.N. 1995. Using stand density index to regulate stocking in uneven-aged stands. In: O'Hara, K., ed. Uneven-aged management-opportunities, constraints and methodologies. Missoula, MT: Montana Forest and Conservation Experiment Station: 110-122.

Ohmann, J.L.; Gregory, M.J. 2002. Predictive mapping of forest composition and structure with direct gradient analysis and nearest-neighbor imputation in coastal Oregon, U.S.A. Canadian Journal of Forest Research. 32:725-741.

Pearson, R.G.; Dawson, T.P. 2003. Predicting the impacts of climate change on distribution of species: are bioclimate envelope models useful? Global Ecology and Biogeography. 12:361-371.

Pierce, K.B.; Ohmann, J.L.; Wimberly, M.C.; Gregory, M.J.; Fried, J.S. 2009. Mapping wildland fuels and forest structure for land management: a comparison of nearest neighbor imputation and other methods. Canadian Journal of Forest Research. 39:1901-1916.

Powell, J.A.; Logan, J.A.; Bentz, B.J. 1996. Local projections for a global model for mountain pine beetle attacks. Journal of Theoretical Biology. 179:243-260.

Powell, J.A.; Bentz, B.J. 2009. Connecting phenological predictions with population growth rates for mountain pine beetle, an outbreak insect. Landscape Ecology. 24:657-672.

R Development Core Team. 2010. R: a language and environment for statistical computing. Vienna: R Foundation for Statistical Computing.

Reineke, L.H. 1933. Perfecting a stand-density index for even-aged forest. Journal of Agricultural Research. 46:627-638.

Ruefenacht, B.; Finco, M.V.; Nelson, M.D.; [and others]. 2008. Conterminous U.S. and Alaska forest type mapping using forest inventory and analysis data. Photogrammetric Engineering & Remote Sensing. 74(11):1379-1388.

Safranyik, L.; Carroll, A.L.; Régnière, J.; Langor, D.W.; Riel, W.G.; Shore, T.L.; Peter, B.; Cooke, B.J.; Nealis, V.G.; Taylor, S.W. 2010. Potential for range expansion of mountain pine beetle into the boreal forest of North America. The Canadian Entomologist. 142(5):415-442.

Savolainen, O.; Pyhajarvi, T.; Knurr, T. 2007. Gene flow and local adaptation in trees. Annual Review of Ecology, Evolution and Systematics. 38:595-619.

U.S. Department of Agriculture Forest Service [USDA], Forest Health Protection. 2005. Aerial survey geographic information system handbook: sketchmaps to digital geographic information. 27 p.

U.S. Department of Agriculture Forest Service, Forest Inventory and Analysis [FIA]. 2004. Forest Inventory and Analysis national core field guide, volume 1: field data collection procedures for phase 2 plots, version 2.0. Washington, DC. 118 p. plus appendices.

U.S. Department of the Interior, Geological Survey [USGS]. 2009. LANDFIRE National Existing Vegetation Type layer (LF_1.0.0), [Online]. Available: http://landfire.cr.usgs.gov/viewer/ [2010, October 28].

Vogelmann, J.E.; Howard, S.M.; Yang, L.; Larson, C.R.; Wylie, B.K.; Van Driel, N. 2001. Completion of the 1990s national land cover data set for the conterminous United States from Landsat thematic mapper data and ancillary data sources. Photogrammetric Engineering & Remote Sensing. 67:650-662.

White, P.; Powell J. 2008. Phase transition from environmental to dynamic determinism in mountain pine beetle attack. Bulletin of Mathematical Biology. 59:609-643.

Wiens, J.A. 1989. Spatial scaling in ecology. Functional Ecology. 3:385-397.

Wood, D.L. 1982. The role of pheromones, kairomones, and allomones in the host selection and colonization behavior of bark beetles. Annual Review of Entomology. 27:411-446.

Woodall, C.W.; Fiedler, C.E.; Milner, K.S. 2003. Stand density index in uneven-aged ponderosa pine stands. Canadian Journal of Forest Research. 33:96-100.

www.ingramcontent.com/pod-product-compliance
Lightning Source LLC
Chambersburg PA
CBHW081125280526
45787CB00007B/2977